Evelyn Cecil

Notes of My Journey Round the World

Evelyn Cecil

Notes of My Journey Round the World

ISBN/EAN: 9783744798266

Printed in Europe, USA, Canada, Australia, Japan

Cover: Foto ©Andreas Hilbeck / pixelio.de

More available books at **www.hansebooks.com**

Photographed by WM. NOTMAN & SON, Montreal
Rocky Mountains: View from Banff Hotel, looking down the Bow Valley
By permission

NOTES OF

MY JOURNEY
ROUND THE WORLD

BY

EVELYN CECIL, B.A.

WITH FIFTEEN FULL-PAGE ILLUSTRATIONS

LONDON
LONGMANS, GREEN, AND CO.
AND NEW YORK: 15 EAST 16th STREET
1889

PREFACE.

IT NEEDS SOME APOLOGY to add one more book to the library already published about journeys round the world; and could I not plead the excuse of having been persuaded to stray from the commendable paths of 'masterly inactivity,' it certainly would have never been written. But this is not intended to be a volume of thrilling adventures or of tales profusely drawing upon the imagination; it is rather a volume of fact, briefly describing things as they exist, and its aim (if not too great a presumption) is to hint at just so much information as may entice the reader into following up any fancy in some larger work.

The journey, in company with my father, through Canada, the States, Japan, Canton, Hong Hong, Singapore, Java, Ceylon, India, and Egypt, took a day or two more than seven months and a half, and I can therefore scarcely expect that notes taken of it will be absolutely free from the inevitable accompaniment of all rapid travelling—a tendency to generalise inaccurately from events or circumstances which have only been seen once. Perhaps, too, some of the descriptions may appear tedious and overdrawn, or interesting only to persons who have visited the reality; but an advantage of longer descriptions over short ones often is that they leave a better general impression, a more representative picture, than any terser summary can ever hope for.

Lastly, I should be glad here to express my grateful thanks to all the authorities we met for the hospitality and kindness which they showed us, without which it would have been quite impossible to have enjoyed so much, or to have accomplished it in so short a time.

E. C.

LYTCHETT HEATH, POOLE:
Jan. 8, 1880.

CONTENTS.

CHAPTER		PAGE
I.	THROUGH THE EASTERN STATES AND CANADA	1
II.	IN THE STATES: THE WILD WEST	27
III.	JAPAN: THE NEIGHBOURHOOD OF YOKOHAMA AND TOKIO	53
IV.	JAPAN: KOBÉ TO KIOTO AND NAGASAKI	77
V.	HONG KONG; CANTON; SINGAPORE; JAVA	93
VI.	CEYLON AND SOUTHERN INDIA	117
VII.	NORTHERN INDIA: FROM CALCUTTA TO DELHI	134
VIII.	NORTHERN INDIA: DELHI TO THE KHYBER PASS; UMRITSUR TO BOMBAY	158
IX.	HOMEWARDS THROUGH ADEN, CAIRO, AND ALEXANDRIA	189

LIST OF ILLUSTRATIONS.

ROCKY MOUNTAINS: VIEW FROM BANFF HOTEL, LOOKING DOWN THE BOW VALLEY	*Frontispiece*
AMERICAN FALLS; NIAGARA	*To face page* 12
ROCKY MOUNTAINS: KICKING HORSE PASS, LOOKING EAST	,, 20
IN THE SELKIRKS; HERMIT RANGE	,, 23
CURRECANTI NEEDLE, ON THE DENVER AND RIO GRANDE RAILROAD	,, 31
CATHEDRAL ROCKS; YOSEMITE VALLEY	,, 37
AVENUE OF CRYPTOMERIAS NEAR NIKKO, JAPAN	,, 65
TORII AND PAGODA AT THE ENTRANCE TO THE SHINTO TEMPLE, NIKKO	,, 68
OUTER ARCHWAY TO SHRINE OF SHINTO TEMPLE, NIKKO	,, 70
MOUNT FUJI; JAPAN	,, 74
STREET IN A JAPANESE VILLAGE	,, 82
VIEW OF MOUNT SALAK FROM BUITENZORG, JAVA	,, 108
THE GREAT PAGODA; TANJORE, SOUTHERN INDIA	,, 129
THE TAJ; AGRA	,, 153
KUTUB MINÁR, NEAR DELHI	,, 163

NOTES

OF MY

JOURNEY ROUND THE WORLD.

CHAPTER I.

THROUGH THE EASTERN STATES AND CANADA.

To four years of University life there is, perhaps, no better antidote than a journey round the world. It is a time especially favourable for receiving new and vivid impressions, and one when there is more leisure to be disposed of than perhaps may be wished for hereafter. Preparations for the start are always an effort; but, once started, matters seem to arrange themselves, and the annoyances or disappointments of the moment soon fade away in the more pleasing recollections of the past.

In sailing for New York towards the end of August, on a journey which is to occupy about seven months and a half, there is still some danger of meeting with that enervating heat which is there so unbearable throughout the summer. The glories of the harbour of the 'Empire City'

B

are, however, if possible, enhanced by the seven days of dreary sea, during which, perchance, the appearance of an iceberg may alleviate the monotony of their daily routine. On the right of the ship, as she enters the harbour, is Coney Island, a favourite bathing-place, quite covered with palatial hotels, of which the latest has assumed the form and colour of an enormous elephant! and behind it is Long Island; while on the left the green hills of Staten Island are almost buried in luxuriant woods. Every incoming steamer has an excellent view of the gigantic bronze statue of Liberty, not long ago erected in the centre of the inner bay; and in the distance Brooklyn Suspension Bridge is no imposture in respect of its far-famed reputation as a masterpiece of modern engineering.

New York is the very essence of a great metropolis of the Western Continent. Its large buildings and crowded streets, its anxious, hurried faces, its busy thoroughfares, whose rutted condition is a melancholy sacrifice to the universal tram-car, and its countless telegraph-poles, are all familiar to those who have been there; but perhaps its elevated railroads are the most peculiar of its enterprising peculiarities. They answer the purpose of our District Railway in London, but are raised in the streets on an elevated iron framework, so that trains run on a level with the first floors of the neighbouring houses. The householders must cordially detest them; yet their airy position makes them much more profitable and popular than our 'Underground' ever could be. The rectangular streets of New York are common to all American cities, and their huge advertisements give ample scope for the brilliancy of American wit.

Passing on to Philadelphia, by far its most interesting feature is Independence Hall, where the representatives of the thirteen original States signed the Declaration of Independence on July 4, 1776. Ever since that memorable day, the Fourth of July has been a great national holiday in the States; and whenever a new State is admitted to the Union, another star is added to the Stars and Stripes on the following Fourth of July. In reading through a copy of the Declaration, it is very evident that its authors had constantly before them the provisions of the Bill of Rights and Act of Settlement; but Washington himself did not sign it, although it contains the signatures of Hancock, Jefferson, Franklin, and others. The Congress of the Union sat in Independence Hall at Philadelphia between 1775 and 1781, when it was removed to Washington.

Apart from seeing the President's White

House, every visitor to Washington goes to the Capitol, which combines under one roof the Senate, the House of Representatives, and the Supreme Court. Its imposing exterior is built in Grecian architecture, so common to the public offices of the United States, and centres in a handsome dome. The interior is decorated with gilt and marble; but every room has a weighty and massive appearance, and must be very depressing to hard-worked legislators. For a session, which lasts from December till March, the members of both Houses receive $5,000 a year (about 1,040*l.*); in England we are so fortunate as to possess unpaid politicians who work nearly three times as hard.

There is no better way of leaving New York than by the daily steamer up the Hudson to Albany. For the first twenty miles an enormous mass of basaltic rock, known as the 'Palisades,' guards the western bank of the river, while magnificent woods overlook the water from the opposite side. During fifteen miles more, the river expands to a width of nearly four miles to form Tappan Bay, which displays a truly striking contrast between the overpowering splendour of an American river and the modest windings of our little Thames. Then the steamer passes Donderberg Mountain and Anthony's Nose, two thickly wooded promontories at one end of the Hudson 'Highlands,' whose lofty fastnesses extend along its banks like colossal recollections of Scotland; and, among these, jutting out upon the pretty headland of West Point, is situated the joint Sandhurst and Woolwich of the United States. On leaving the Highlands the scenery becomes tamer, until the Catskill Mountains, the mythical abode of Rip van Winkle, appear on the western bank; but, farther up, the stream narrows down to comparatively moderate proportions, which would not be navigable but for the Government dykes, and on its brink large ice store-houses are conspicuous and ugly.

From Albany to Montreal is a night's journey by railway, concluding with the great Victoria Bridge over the St. Lawrence—almost the longest in the world, for it has twenty-five arches, and is over a mile and a half long. It is built entirely of iron, 8,000 tons of it having been used in its construction; and its whole length consists of a tunnel, through which the trains of the Grand Trunk Railway take about four or five minutes to run. It was formally opened by the Prince of Wales in 1860, and was made in the shape of a tunnel from an idea that the snow in the winter would not then cause it so much damage as might be the case with an open bridge—a mistake only now being discovered, when the rusty iron is in need of constant repair.

The most precipitous side of Mount Royal, at the background of Montreal, can be climbed in about two minutes by an elevator or steam-lift, a mode of ascent as safe and ingenious as at first sight it seems strange; and once at the top there is a wide view over the town and the St. Lawrence.

While at Montreal, also, an excursion is invariably made to shoot the Lachine Rapids on the St. Lawrence. They are about seven miles above the town, and two below the village of Lachine, and in summer steamers paddle down them every day. As they are approached, the large and numerous eddies of the river become every minute more formidable; and the excitement at the moment of shooting them is only equal to one's interest in watching the steamer as it darts through the waves and avoids the half-submerged rocks, which considerably exercise the ingenuity of the steersman.

Down the St. Lawrence it is easy in twelve hours to reach Quebec, whose citadel and old city-walls (for it is the only walled city in America) lend an additional charm to its beautiful site. On the south the citadel shuts out the town from the historic plains of Abraham, where General Wolfe's monument, with its significant inscription, 'Here died Wolfe victorious: Sept. 13, 1759,' tells its own tale. From the Durham and Dufferin Terrace, just under the citadel, there is a very fine panorama (looking over the St. Lawrence) of the distant Beauport Mountains, whose harmony and softness it would be difficult to excel; but it is far too extensive to be reproduced with justice in any sketch or photograph.

The Protestant cathedral is large, but has no pretension to beauty, having been built in the time of George III. In it there is a monument to Dr. Jacob Mountain, the first Anglican bishop, about whom an amusing anecdote is told. King George is said to have expressed some hesitation, in the presence of Dr. Mountain, as to whom to appoint bishop of the new See of Quebec. The Doctor answered, 'If your Majesty had faith, there would be no difficulty.' 'How so?' said the King. 'If you had faith,' replied Mountain, 'you would say to this Mountain, "Be thou removed into that See," and it would be done.' The witticism won him the appointment.

The streets of Quebec are often steep and rugged, and the large number of French names, advertisements, and translations points to the fact that about three quarters of the population are French Canadians.

The Parliament House is spacious and neat, and its interior is a great improvement upon that of the Capitol at Washington. It is, of course, merely the local parliament of the province of

Quebec, and is quite distinct from the Dominion Parliament which meets at Ottawa. In the Legislative Council, or Upper House, of the Quebec province there are twenty-four members, appointed for life by nomination of the Crown through the Lieutenant-Governor of Quebec. The Legislative Assembly, or Lower House, consists of sixty-five members, elected by constituencies as in England; but no parliament may sit for more than five years. The members receive only 600 dollars a year (125$l.$), besides their travelling expenses; and at present their number in the Lower House averages about five Frenchmen to one Englishman; each member may speak in whichever language he prefers, and the debates are published both in English and French.

Eight miles from Quebec are the Falls of Montmorenci; and though the Montmorenci river contains but little water, it is so uniformly distributed over the precipitous rock that the falls are among the finest in America. They are 50 feet wide and 250 feet high, and as the glistening spray floats over the stream below, it forms, as it were, a very beautiful network of gossamer.

The Parliament House at Ottawa is a well-designed group of buildings—indeed, there are at present few other large erections in the town—and it is in the main or central block that both the

Senate and House of Commons hold their sessions. The former consists of seventy-eight members, nominated by the Crown through the Governor General for life; in the latter there are 215 elected members. The session begins at the end of January, and lasts about three months.

Ottawa is a night's journey from Toronto— in its ways a very English city, and accordingly most appropriately situated between two York shire rivers, the Don and the Humber. There are in it, besides, fewer of the French Canadians, who keep so much aloof from the English population in Montreal and Quebec. It has no very special attractions; but during a spare moment there is time to look into Osgoode Hall, the law courts of the town, and listen to the proceedings of the Appeal Court. Two of the practising counsel there have actually resigned their seats on the bench of judges, on account of the low salaries which the bench receive; and the cases are very deplorable, inasmuch as new judges are unconsciously apt to treat the remarks of these counsel with undue deference. Fortunately there are no other such instances at the Canadian bar.

On a dark and still September evening, about eight o'clock, there is something romantic in approaching Niagara, and arriving within hearing of the ceaseless roar of its tremendous cataract.

It is a picture too hopeless to contemplate, too surpassing in majesty, to allow any true idea of its vivid magnificence. Whether you go before the falls or behind them, beneath them or around them, their overwhelming grandeur seems never to diminish. A mile above them, the Niagara river spreads out into foaming rapids, whose fury would be imposing in any other spot, and leaves behind it various islets, of which the Three Sister Islands, Luna Island, and Goat Island are the most important. The last is by far the largest, and divides at its lower end the Horse-shoe or Canadian falls from those on the American side. The Canadian falls are 156 feet high and 2,300 broad; the American are 164 feet high and about 1,300 broad. They are, of course, quite indescribable. As the raging water dashes down the precipice, with a force which nothing can oppose, into the surging sea below, and forms in the rays of sunlight bright clouds of dazzling spray, it is hard to conceive in nature a more perfect embodiment of irresistible might and power. From the Clifton Suspension Bridge the water glides on in calmer eddies (the river being here about 1,200 feet wide), with no warning of a fresh disturbance until it reaches the two bridges of the Michigan Central and Grand Trunk Railways, a few hundred yards below. Here, however, the gorge narrows to about 300 feet, and the great pressure of the water above causes the most violent rapids, the waves of which are literally more than rivals of a stormy Atlantic. They extend down the river for three-quarters of a mile, and are no less than 250 feet deep, while the rocks on either side are 240 feet high. At the end of the rapids there is a great whirlpool, 400 feet deep, which gives its name to the 'Whirlpool' rapids above. Its waters look comparatively calm and seductive; but its smooth surface conceals a dangerous undercurrent, whose powers of suction are very fatal. The outlet to the whirlpool is at right angles to the original stream, and is the narrowest and deepest part of the whole river, being only 296 feet wide, but nearly 500 feet deep. From this point to Lake Ontario the river flows a distance of twelve miles.

The little steamer 'Maid of the Mist' is always ready to convey passengers as near as is possible to the foot of both the American and Horse-shoe falls. By landing on the American side, one can make one's way more easily over the Upper Rapids to Goat Island, from which there is a descent to the so-called Cave of the Winds, where the sensation experienced is far more wonderful than that under the falls on the Canadian side. The cave is merely a deep curve in the rock, exactly under the left side (as the river flows) of the American falls, and a special suit of flannel and waterproof is necessary to enter it. Venturing on, with the customary guide, the driving spray suddenly becomes so blinding that the rock which forms one's path is scarcely visible; but, on emerging from the cave, small wooden bridges lead round over the rocks to the front of the fall, where beautifully complete and tiny circles of the rainbow are glistening in several crannies. This general effect just in front of the falling water is perhaps the most impressive of all, and a more perfect realisation of the beauty and majesty which is so true a feature of every inch of Niagara.

It is well worth one's while to 'contemplate' Niagara for a day or two. Even when, at first sight, one's expectations have been unreasonable and cause a slight disappointment, the falls grow more fascinating every hour, and every visitor must admit before long that their grandeur is indeed unrivalled.

Perhaps after Niagara everything is imbued with a kind of tameness; but a farm among the backwoods of Eastern Canada is certainly of more than ordinary interest, although, were it not for the absence of hedges, its cultivated grounds are not very dissimilar to those in England. In the woods in autumn, the glorious crimson red of the

maples is the crowning beauty of every forest; but there is a novelty in the variety of trees, which makes them suggestive of a perpetual English shrubbery. They comprise numbers of white cedars, of bass-wood (in appearance very like a lime-tree, and a useful white wood for furniture), moose-wood (a shrub formerly much used by the Indians for tying knots), hemlock-spruce, iron-wood, white-ash, and Canadian pine. The farmers, however, of Eastern Canada can make but little profit, since they are now being inevitably outbidden by the virgin soil of the West. They live very thriftily, and employ few labourers, for labour is very dear both in Canada and the States, and their wives and children are ever ready to help them in the very commonest and roughest work.

From enjoying the hospitality of so pleasant a country visit it is rather dismal to return to large towns like Chicago, remarkable only for their business and their size, and also, with all due deference, for the uncompromising pride with which their inhabitants regard them. The newly-built Minneapolis is as neat and clean as any of them, and is pleasantly situated on undulating ground. On its outskirts there are some pretty woods and lakes, while in the centre of the town the Mississippi divides itself into two channels, which flow round Nicollet Island. The fall of water is here very considerable, and the water-power (to which Minneapolis mainly owes its existence) is mostly used for flour-mills and iron-foundries; among which, with characteristic Yankee self-assurance, Pillsbury's flour-mill claims in its advertisements to be the eighth wonder of the world.

Retreating northwards again to Canada, Winnipeg now flourishes in the midst of wide and well-paved streets: and several large buildings, which have all grown up in the last six years, evidently show that it is a rising town and anxious to become a large city. Its position as the capital of Manitoba, and the focus of an extensive agricultural district, certainly augurs well for its future ambitions.

All round Winnipeg lies a vast prairie, with not even an apology for rising ground from which to get a good general view of the town; and, as it flows through it, the Red River appears as an ordinary-sized, sluggish, and muddy stream, shut in by the most unattractive banks. Autumn weather in Winnipeg is delightful during the day; but the difference in temperature at night is incredible, and often, at first, rather trying. In winter the thermometer goes down to about $-40°$ Fahr. (seventy degrees of frost!) and although the snow is not usually more than three inches deep, the farmers are shut in with no occupation but to feed their cattle, and undergo a kind of enforced idleness which is easily productive of regrettable consequences.

Through the kindness of a most courteous gentleman near Winnipeg an opportunity may arise of seeing his herd of tame buffalo, or more properly bisons, which he keeps about twelve miles from the town. These splendid animals condescend to receive visitors at a distance of twenty yards, and their handsome heads and sparkling eyes are indeed a picture of magnificence and strength. If chased on horseback, the buffalo is not slow to prove that, although he may seem heavy and slothful when he is at rest, he can bolt much faster than a galloping horse. The tame herd wanders over a prairie nine miles by eight in size.

It is very melancholy that no wild buffaloes are now believed to exist in North America. They have all been persecuted by railways, or exterminated by the wanton and ruthless destruction formerly practised upon them by Indian, and more recently by American sportsmen; and, though their disappearance is everywhere lamented, no amount of remorse can bring them back. In Norway a recent law has stringently preserved the game before it is too late: may we in England also learn the lesson which America teaches!

In leaving Winnipeg by the Canadian Pacific

Railway the journey towards the Wild West is fairly begun. As the train glides on through the long prairie grass, or halts at a newly built town which seems to fix the future market of some flourishing district, the landscape is continually dotted with prairie farms or distant cattle. And such farmers have at present a very enviable prospect. Their industry, however, must not be nominal, and they must not start with a capital of less than 500*l.* They should not be up later than six in the morning, nor shoot when they ought to be at work. Suppose, in such a case, that wheat in Manitoba sells at sixty cents (2*s.* 6*d.*) a bushel, or 20*s.* a quarter, and that it would fetch at Liverpool 34*s.* a quarter, a hard-working farmer can ensure a profit of over twenty per cent. under ordinary circumstances, even after taking into account his primary outlay in erecting a house and outbuildings, buying seed, implements, and other necessaries, and his maintenance for the first year. His advantages over an English farmer are in respect of rent, rates, and taxes, original cost of the freehold (which is about two and a half dollars, or 10*d.* 6*d.*, per acre), and the wheat itself, for the soil in Manitoba and Assiniboia now produces the very best. Labour costs on an average one and a half dollars a day, or thirty-six shillings a week, as opposed to fourteen shillings a week in England; but the labourers work harder, and work by the piece and not by the hour; and the farmer directs all the work himself, without a thought of employing an agent or foreman.

The prairie rolls on towards Calgary and the Rocky Mountains in low, undulating hills, the home of the 'coyote,' or prairie-dog, and, more especially in winter, the antelope; or it dips down in graceful curves to small lakelets, sometimes fresh, sometimes alkaline, abounding with geese and duck, which start away in black clouds as they are disturbed in turn by the approaching train. At the stations several Red Indians, squaws, and papooses, arrayed in bright-coloured rugs, and vain in proportion to the paint on their faces, figure upon the platform. They are usually the refuse of their tribe, and intent upon selling buffalo-horns, for they have found out that many a traveller falls an easy victim to their persuasions.

Where the railway crosses the South Saskatchewan—a region of rattlesnakes—it is very refreshing to see the oaks and poplars which skirt its banks, for scarcely a tree has been visible during the thirty hours' journey from Winnipeg. There is then a steep ascent from the Saskatchewan to the fine prairie above, which is all part of the ranch country, intersected with buffalo-trails, and covered with semi-circular depressions, marking the former wallows of these prairie kings.

After entering the territory of Alberta, at a spot where there spring out jets of natural gas, some of which are often lighted to speed the passing train, its capital at Calgary is soon reached, and affords an excellent halting-place before journeying on through the Rockies. It is well situated within sight of their soft grey and jagged peaks, and stands on a plateau encircled by low hills, with the ripple of the Bow and Elbow Rivers close by—an admirable position for an increasing trade. The land round Calgary is very favourable to agriculture, and, since very little corn can be grown *in* the Rockies, it may soon be expected to become the metropolis for feeding their advancing population, as well as the connecting link between Eastern and Western Canada. It is a wonderful instance of the erection of a complete town in three or four years; though its grassy streets and somewhat unfinished look still tend to betray its recent growth. Its climate is generally good. The severity of the winter lasts only from December to February, when the frosts are tremendous, though there falls but little snow—a circumstance which renders ranching practicable near Calgary, while it is almost unknown in Manitoba. The industrious ranchmen seem to lead a very enjoyable life, if not too rough a one; they live in their saddles, and require only health, opportunity, and a little common sense to make a good business of their horses.

Throughout this district Indians and Indian wigwams are very common. The Blackfeet and the Crees are the two chief tribes of Western Canada; the Ojibbeway Indians are scattered over Eastern Canada, and the Sioux Indians are natives of the United States. All Indian tribes speak totally different languages, being unable to understand each other; and an experienced eye can at once tell their features apart. On making treaties with the various tribes, the Canadian Government has allowed each tribe to choose its own 'reserve,' or large tract of land, which was in future to be its residence. Conditionally on their retiring to this reserve, the Government allow the Indians so many dollars a day according to their rank among themselves, so that now they are really dependent upon the Government for their food and maintenance. But, alas! a quiet, half-civilised life ill agrees with their spirited constitution, and they seem to be gradually dying out and wasting away through the ravages of consumption and fever.

From Calgary to the Rocky Mountains the line follows the valley of the Bow, and winds among the foot-hills, whose thirty miles of graceful slopes are fit heralds to the shaggy heights beyond.

At 'the Gap,' the entrance to the Rockies, the novelty of the scene is truly grand. All round are rocky peaks of every shape, at whose bases the dark green spruce contrasts strikingly in autumn with the pale yet glowing yellow of the birch or poplar; while beneath the river Bow trickles quietly on, washed with the greenish hue of glacier streams. At Banff the hot sulphur springs, in the midst of bracing mountain air, promise before long to become a fashionable resort; for, in the cave of sulphur water at one side of the Sulphur Mountain, the temperature is extremely pleasant, and the curious yellow deposits and crystallised walls are quite romantic surroundings for a morning's swim. A visit to the Devil's Lake has also many charms.

Beyond Banff the views grow grander and grander, and each fresh turn in the railway has the varying effect of a vast kaleidoscope. Sometimes the train runs through a dark forest of Canadian pine, which lines the borders of some wandering rivulet, and is enclosed by two rows of rocky battlements and fantastic, snowy tops; sometimes it creeps along the cliffs of a dizzy spur, which overhangs a mountain lake or the precipitous valley of some foaming torrent, as it leaps far away into the depths below. Presently another range looms out in a vista of endless peaks,

till all of a sudden these are hidden by bold and jutting rocks, which lead the railway into a narrow gorge, and force it to cross and recross the gurgling stream : and at last it emerges from a rocky gateway, to come in full view of the blue Columbia. The Columbia valley is here most enchanting. In front gleam out the Selkirks, clear against the azure sky, the unrivalled kings of every range, on whose silvery crests and cedar-clad foot-hills the lights and shadows are too magnificent to describe. Below, the banks of the river are clothed in tints of every shade; and behind, the Rockies stand out as no mean partners in the scene. After crossing the Columbia a steep ascent begins over the Selkirks, where the railway, unlike its windings through the Rockies, lies straight up the mountain, spanning deep ravines, and leaving bright cascades to dash far beneath amid a sea of firs. At Rogers' Pass the frowning heights of Mount Carroll overlook the train. It is indeed a majestic mountain, towering just a mile above the rail, with its slopes entwined in glaciers; and it is doubtless owing to the nearness of its stupendous precipice that it seems to convey a keener sense of the Rockies' individual grandeur than does any other of their lofty heights. Just beyond it is the Glacier House, a pretty Swiss chalet, built as an hotel by the Canadian Pacific

Railway Company, and presided over by the noble peak of Sir Donald.

The Glacier House is only two miles from the foot of the Sir Donald Glacier, melted last year into a deep, icy cave, stretching some forty feet into the ice, and measuring from ten to fifteen feet high. From its pale blue walls and thick transparent ceiling two arches formed an outlet, both resting upon a massive icy pillar, and each carved into crystal points. From these the melted water dripped slowly upon the stony floor; while each arch disclosed a green slope of distant trees, all the more beautiful in the setting sun, and almost like a glimpse of some other world from the glassy palaces of fairyland.

To climb the glacier needs a guide and a hard day's work. The first four miles from the Glacier House pass through a forest of spruces, and along the banks of a milky torrent, where a rifle is always a useful companion should one chance to meet a bear. It is a favourite haunt of black bears, but cinnamons and the more dangerous grizzlies are not so often at home. The next mile is a weary ascent, at the end of which all signs of verdure are left behind, and the road becomes a monotonous trudge through heavy boulders of loose rock. Higher up, the region of glacial mud proves the most difficult part of the journey; and

beyond it the climb is intercepted by one or two narrow crevasses: and impregnable parapets of ice show themselves off to their best advantage, indented with streaks of pale transparent blue, or deeply worn away into wrinkled ledges. The highest part of the glacier is about 11,000 feet above the sea.

Soon after leaving the Glacier House, the railway track takes the form of great curves or loops, from the first of which it is actually visible one hundred feet lower down, at a spot where the train arrives in a few minutes. Here, again, there is a most splendid view, in the very heart of the Selkirks. On the left the handsome outline of Ross Peak peers out in solitary grandeur, while looking back over the wild gorge of the Ille-cille-waet stream, the snowy satellites of Sir Donald cluster round his stately pyramid. The mountain forests are the abode of bears and mountain goat; the neighbouring district is full of mineral ore, though the gold and silver mines are not very effectively worked at present. After passing perpendicular gorges and deep abysses, the line re-crosses the Columbia, and leads up by the creeks and lakes of the Gold Range to the town of Kamloops, one of the oldest western settlements of the Hudson's Bay Company; but the scenery here is not to be compared with that in the Selkirks, and the surrounding hills are covered with a short brownish grass, which gives the country a very desolate and arid appearance. The town is situated at the 'confluence of two rivers,' whence its Indian name, and a few miles below it these rivers widen out into the Kamloops Lake.

From this point to Vancouver the finest views are along the canyon or gorge of the Fraser River. Every day the single mail train arrives there towards early dawn, when heavy veils of floating mist still fringe the mountain-tops; but even in the twilight each ray sparkles over the foam, and shines with a silvery glitter from off the whirlpools below. Near the approach to North Bend, the Fraser canyon becomes more and more striking, with its walls of graceful mountains and luxuriance of gigantic trees, which are if possible improved by the varied colouring of the shrubs. All these converge towards the rocky fortresses which guard the channel of the eddying river, and unite to form a most enchanting picture, and a very lovely type of the beauties of British Columbia.

Towards Vancouver and along the coast there flourish great numbers of the enormous Douglas firs for which British Columbia is famous. Many of them are no less than 250 feet high; but their roots are so large and indestructible that it is not worth while, when they have been cut down, to break up the ground for purposes of farming or pasture, and it may therefore be doubted whether Vancouver will ever grow to be an agricultural centre. Owing to its position on the continent, while Victoria (the capital of British Columbia) is on Vancouver Island, its friends have hopes that it will supplant that city; but its prospects seem chiefly to depend upon its capacity as a commercial port, and upon its being the present and only terminus of the Canadian Pacific Railway. How far these advantages are the germs of complete success may be matter for consideration. As a high road for the trade of Great Britain with Hong Kong and China, the cost and risks of transhipment will always detract from its utility, although the actual time of passage, as compared with that through the Bay of Biscay and Indian Ocean, may be a trifle less: on the other hand, it is certain that an influx of population into Western Canada will largely increase the importance of Vancouver. It is, as we have mentioned, the present terminus of the Canadian Pacific: but should any causes, whether commercial, engineering, or political, create a rival harbour, the blow would be a cruel one to that well-deserving and pioneering town.

The Canadian Pacific Railway trains run through from Montreal to Vancouver in less than six days. Their cars are very comfortably and handsomely fitted up, and the dining-cars, which are unknown on many southern American lines, make travellers independent of refreshment stations, and secure them a good and punctual meal even if the train should happen to be late. The rails appear well-laid, notwithstanding their rapid construction, and the only requirements now wanting are population and traffic. The wheat-fields of Manitoba and the minerals of the Rocky Mountains have suddenly been made easily accessible, and, if the energy of the promoters is rewarded as it deserves, it is to be hoped that ample returns will soon be forthcoming.

From Vancouver to Victoria a steamer takes about six hours to go through the pretty archipelago of wooded islands and the Straits of Georgia, where numbers of small whales persistently advertise themselves by frolics and spoutings. The excellent English aspect of Victoria is unique; and its climate, always agreeable and never very cold, seems to suit the coveys of Californian quail which have been introduced there, and which afford a very pleasant day's shooting, together with pheasants, a kind of grouse, and sometimes even a deer. Three miles away is the great dockyard of Esquimalt, an efficient and valuable retreat for our Pacific Squadron; and further north the district of Nanaimo is very rich in coal.

CHAPTER II.

IN THE STATES: THE WILD WEST.

LEAVING the pleasures of Canada, and crossing the Straits of San Juan de Fuca, the daily steamer passes down Puget Sound to land at the new town of Tacoma in Washington Territory,[1] which is the terminus of a line of railway through Portland to Salt Lake City. At Kaláma the line is interrupted by the Columbia, there about a mile in width; and as the construction of a bridge would have been onerously expensive, American ingenuity has not been at a loss to find some better method of transit. The whole train is actually

---

[1] A territory (*e.g.* Washington Territory, Idaho, Utah, or Indian Territory) differs from a state in several particulars. It does not send representatives to Congress, but only 'delegates' or assessors, who are expected to watch over its interests, but cannot take part in debates. It does not pay taxes to the Federal Government; and, as its inhabitants are not United States citizens, they have no votes in a Presidential election. Like a state, it has two (local) legislative assemblies; but, unlike it, its governor is selected by the President of the United States, and not appointed by itself. When sufficiently civilised or populated, a territory may be admitted to be a state by the vote of its inhabitants, accepted by President and Congress.

ferried across the river in a large boat, which is worked by steam and paddle-wheels, and can carry, on a centre line and two sidings, no less than three trains at once. The invention was only made about four years ago.

Salt Lake City is situated in a plain, amidst brown but picturesque hills, and enjoys a temperature neither too hot in summer nor too cold in winter. It looks a clean, quiet, and orderly town, with broad streets and promising avenues; and it is protected and watched, in case of disturbance, by the military post of Fort Douglas, three miles away. It is as much as eighteen miles from the Great Salt Lake, to which there runs a rather capricious railway.

But it is chiefly interesting as the home of the Mormons, who make up about five-sevenths of the population of 26,000, and are, as a rule, a very industrious and peaceable society. Yet they do not just now make many converts. A chance of attending one of the half-yearly conferences in the Mormon tabernacle is a golden opportunity for observing their ceremonies. The tabernacle is a long, low, oval erection, fitted for some 12,000 people, and is a temporary substitute for the unwieldy Mormon temple, which has been building for thirty-five years, and still remains unfinished. Its decorations consist only of a fine organ at one end, and ten-year-old evergreens, or rather skeleton festoons hung from the roof. Immediately below the organ are seated an immense choir, men on one side, and women on the other ; and below them are a row of pews, each one above the last, and each centering in a small pulpit, where the various grades of apostles, high councillors, and bishops sit or preach to the assembly. Elders and deacons have apparently no special pew. The functionaries wear ordinary clothes, and conversation seems to be indifferently allowed both before and during the service. The music is effective and the singing good; but the preaching, which always predominates, is very suggestive of a fanatical Hyde Park oration, and one cannot forget that the preachers at the conference are the lights of the Mormon Church. The audience, as might be supposed, are ignorant, credulous, and illiterate—a state of mind quickly proved by questioning almost any one of their number, when his superficial and hesitating knowledge about their prophet, their religion, or their doctrines, is really quite pitiful.

The Mormon creed is a strange imposture. Besides accepting our Old and New Testaments, they believe in the Book of 'Mormon,' a supposed Hebrew prophet, whose writings, engraved on golden tablets, are asserted to have been divinely revealed in 1830 to Joe Smith, the son of a poor farmer, and the prophet and founder of Mormonism. He is said to have learnt in a dream of their hiding-place in New York State, to have translated them into English by the help of two witnesses, one of whom appears afterwards to have quarrelled with him, and in another vision to have restored them to their divine revealer, whose foresight thus prevented their further investigation. By other revelations Joe Smith professes to have been granted the spirit of prophecy, or power of interpreting the Scriptures as directed by his inclinations, and the 'spirit' is also claimed by all his followers, the 'Latter-day Saints.' These outrageous interpretations are cynically advocated on grounds of morality, and foolish persons are deluded into joining a religion which is little else but a counterpart of Christianity, with polygamy as an additional attraction. Baptism is not allowed by Mormons until a child is eight years old, although a person may be baptized by proxy after his death—a mark of respect which may be conferred, we suppose, sometimes even against his will. What, for instance, if George Washington were to be honoured with such a privilege?

The policy of the United States Government in carrying out the suppression of Mormonism seems a very wise one. Persecution can never extinguish fanaticism: while judicious laws cannot fail to

Currecanti Needle, on the Denver and Rio Grande Railroad

have a salutary effect. Among many such restrictions no one may vote, or serve as an officer or juror in Utah, unless he subscribes to an oath or affirmation that he has not infringed the moral provisions of certain Acts.

Although the beauties of the Denver and Rio Grande Railway (which runs through Salt Lake City and Colorado) are not easily exaggerated, it is scarcely pleasant to reach many of them in the dark, owing to the unpunctuality of one's train, to starve with two indifferent meals in twenty-four hours, or to be forced to change carriages at such preposterous times as two and four A.M.; but in America there is often only one passenger train a day, and the public has no escape from the rude tyranny of its conductor. It is at the Black Canyon of the Gunnison that the fine scenery of the line really commences. An open car is tacked on to the end of the train, to give travellers a better view ; and for some twelve miles it steams through wrinkled precipices of red rock, on the very verge of the Gunnison's foaming torrent, passing here and there red rocky and needle-like spires, whose dignity is very prominent and imposing. Presently the railway ascends by wonderful loops and steep gradients to the summit of the Rockies at Marshall's Pass, where its elevation above the sea is no less than

10,858 feet; but the mountains, though very fine, are strewn in autumn with dry and barren turf, and the fir-trees upon them are as often dead as alive. On the right, to the east of Marshall's Pass, rises the handsome form of the Sangre de Cristo range, not far from the lofty peak of Mount Ouray, conspicuous with its snowy top; but here again the brown tufts upon its slopes scarcely harmonise with their graceful outline. On the other side of the pass is the valley and yellow stream of the Arkansas. Its 'Royal Gorge' is second to none; and even in the starlight its grim walls of perpendicular rock are terrible enough, as they tower far above the railway, and are yet so near that there is barely room for the train and the river to pass between them. At every curve, the weird glimmer of the engine tends to make the scene more ghostly, and vivifies its stern reality.

The engineering of the Denver line is at least as wonderful as that on the Canadian Pacific, and its grandest views are quite unrivalled; but, trusting always that one's judgment was not warped by unpunctuality and starvation, its mountains do not seem so rocky or snow-tipped, and its general scenery is not so magnificent, varied, or continuous.

The prairie lands of Colorado and New Mexico are much used for grazing; and occasionally they are dotted with the grey mud-huts of semi-barbarous, indolent Mexicans.

Adjoining them, the wilds of Arizona are partly desert, and partly—on the higher ground—converted into horse, sheep, or cattle ranches; but the population contains some highly unpleasant characters; everybody goes about armed; and murders are committed approximately once a week! Every now and then, near one of the roughest of villages, the sheriff or chief constable of Arizona may be seen taking out for a drive some callous-looking half-breed, one of the few survivors in a skirmish between sheep- and cattle-men. He is a murderer, it is true, but he will generally be let off with a light punishment, for such fights are so frequent in Arizona that they are almost as little noticed as a duel abroad.

The larger ranches in the district have an acreage of perhaps 200 square miles—mostly pine forest—and feed some 5,000 cattle apiece, paying each of their fifteen or twenty cowboys thirty-five to fifty dollars a month (7*l.* to ten guineas). As profitable undertakings, they have been too recently started to have emerged as yet from the realms of speculation, and the cost of carriage along a monopolised railway, even to the nearest market, places them just now at some disadvantage. To many the life might have great attractions, with its chances of sport among deer or antelope; but for an unequestrian visitor, a gallop across the roughnesses of Arizona on a cowboy's pony and in a Mexican saddle, with a Winchester repeater at his side, and an ammunition belt round his waist, the position is more disconcerting. At home, the cowboys' habits are strange ones. They are most civil and hospitable to their guests; but the scarcity of sheets, towels, and apparently water, is very disagreeable to our English notions; and they often sleep in blankets in the open air, even when there is snow on the ground. Their bill of fare is, of course, peculiarly their own. For lunch, some capital beef from the ranch itself, cooked in flour by one of the 'boys,' some excellent bread (a patent of the same expert), raw tomatoes, tinned prunes, and coffee, all contribute to a comfortable meal, which is served up in tin cups and plates, and is quite appropriate to the occasion and to the huts.

Arizona is separated from California by the muddy river Colorado, which is crossed by the railway on a large wooden bridge of sixteen arches; and before reaching it, the sandy desert, abounding in yaccas and various kinds of cactus, is a sure sign of one's approach to semi-tropical regions. While among the heights of the Sierra Nevadas fine swooping eagles sometimes emerge from their secret recesses, but much of the east of California is a lifeless, barren desert, merely from dearth of moisture, for the soil is otherwise good; and it is only further westward that the land becomes more cultivated. At one station, however, a little geyser of cold water plays about four feet high.

The famous Yosemite Valley is sixty-five miles from the nearest railway-station at Raymond, by a rickety mail-coach, and along a dusty road; and it is usual to break the journey about half-way, at the Wawona Hotel. The coach from Raymond soon reaches pretty, undulating country, scattered with ilex, oak, and different bushes, particularly buck-eyes, which are about the size of a large rhododendron, and bear a sandy-coloured, poisonous fruit, something between a pear and a lemon. The small birds, too, seem more plentiful than in many parts of America; and the pale-blue jays attract special attention. While changing horses at Grub Gulch (what a name!) there is time to walk down to the mouth of a small gold-mine; and just beyond, the banks of the hills are fruitful in wild oats. After a further change of horses during lunch at Grant Springs, there begins a fresh ascent, and the scenery becomes gradually grander, while increasing numbers of grey squirrels, mountain and valley quail, and jack rabbits frolic or gambol about. The undulating hills are supplanted by mountains; forests are the substitute for single trees; and gigantic firs, whose trunks and height make them equal to their associates in British Columbia, take the place of the more puny oaks. The hotel at Wawona is 4,000 feet above the sea, and twenty-six miles from the Yosemite Valley.

At Inspiration Point suddenly unfolds the best general view of the Yosemite—on the western slope of the Sierra Nevadas; but, as in a photograph, it fails to convey any adequate idea of the individual awfulness of each precipice in this magnificent vista. It has been said that the valley is indescribable, and certainly it is almost impudent to attempt the description of a gorge whose main portion is five miles long, about one mile wide, and whose every cliff is at least half a mile high. In the foreground on the left the sheer unbroken precipice of El Capitan, unequalled in the world, and 3,300ft. above the valley, commands the entrance to the gorge; but to anyone who has not had the good fortune to see it, its height is inconceivable, and to say that its smooth surface is one-fifth of the size of Mont Blanc is only a very feeble method of hinting any conception of its vastness. Facing it, on the right, stand the Three Graces or Cathedral Rocks, which, in the more rainy seasons, the Bridal Veil Falls bedew with a

Cathedral Rocks, Yosemite Valley

delicate curtain. Behind these, Sentinel Dome and the Sentinel Rock can be seen, and in the background the noble Half-Dome, overshadowed by the peak called Cloud's Rest, is a very superb feature. Each moment, in the descent to the valley, the heights of El Capitan grow more conspicuous and grand; while presently, at the back of the Cathedral Rocks, the two Cathedral Spires stand up erect in their graceful symmetry. Next to them follow Profile Point and the great Sentinel Rock, to whose majestic guardianship the time-honoured Liedig's hotel has been entrusted. Making a tour round the valley, the splendid pines, firs, and Douglas spruces disclose here and there flighty glimpses of the Merced River, as it glides through the midst of the gorge; and soon on the right beyond Sentinel Rock comes Glacier Point (3,200 ft.), whose sloping base from this point of view completely overwhelms its perpendicular top—an optical illusion very curiously reversed when viewed from the top itself. At the end of the main valley, leaving on the right the canyon leading to the Vernal and Nevada Falls, the Merced is crossed on Tissa-ack bridge, where the trees form a handsome framework for a beautiful picture of the North Dome. Under it is Washington Tower, and not far off Mirror Lake; but, owing to want of water, its reflections of all parts of the valley are usually, in autumn, engulfed in mud. Beyond North Dome are the Royal Arches, Eagle Point, the Yosemite Falls, and the Three Brothers, ending again with the stupendous cliff of El Capitan, on whose precipice several natural engravings of human faces have become the very legitimate sources of an Indian legend.

A ride round by the north-east end of the valley to the top of Glacier Point is a most fascinating expedition. The mountainous path along the Merced canyon soon leads into an enormous basin of granite, lined with streaks of fir, whose upper end is graced by the Vernal Falls and the proud hood of the Half-Dome. After crossing and recrossing the Merced, the path winds between the vertical heights of the Cap of Liberty (3,100 ft. above the valley) on the left and the beautiful Nevada Falls (700 ft. deep) on the right; and then abruptly turning round, it leads back through wild azalea-bushes and lofty trees towards the Illilouette Falls and Glacier Point, while the Half-Dome and the less ambitious Cap of Liberty are ever varying in their loveliness.

From Glacier Point the view is too glorious for imagination. It seems here to be divided in two by the Teneyia canyon, the valley which separates the North and Half Domes, with its centre adorned by Mirror Lake. In the view on the left the North Dome and Royal Arches are very striking, and the Yosemite Falls, when there is water in them, are doubtless equally fine. El Capitan is just out of sight. A glimpse over the precipice into the valley, where the Merced meanders along, and the large, newly-building hotel looks the size of a bird-cage, gives some idea of its awful depth of 3,200 ft. On the right the view is yet more imposing; and there the Half-Dome, so accurately sliced, is by far the most commanding figure in the landscape. Below it the Cap of Liberty overshadows the Vernal and Nevada Falls, and on the distant sky-line, amid a maze of sierras, a gleam of snow on Mount Lyell marks the source of the Merced. Still further to the right is the graceful cone of Mount Starr King, encircled by a group of rugged peaks, each vying with the beauty of the last.

But the valley is indeed past all description. Its vertical precipices of granite, more than half a mile high, its glorious domes and fantastic heights, are beyond all imagination, and could hardly be exaggerated even by extravagant anticipations; and, in a space so comparatively small, its peculiar splendour is probably the grandest piece of scenery that any country in the world can at a moment display.

In summer the climate of the Yosemite, which is 4,060 feet above the sea, is very delightful, its season lasting from May 1 to October 31, and the best time for seeing it being about the first of June; but in winter the snow varies in different years from fifteen inches to six feet. All the rocks are of white granite, though occasionally a darker vein has found its way into their midst. In its neighbourhood there are a few cinnamon (brown) and grizzly bears (whence its Indian name, 'Yo-semite' meaning a large grizzly bear), and rattlesnakes have sometimes been seen. Previously to 1851 the valley was scoured by Indians, and no white man had ever entered it. To-day their reserve is some little distance away, and it is mournful to see the few wigwams that represent their former greatness.

There are about seven of the famous big-tree groves scattered throughout California, but the best, as well as the nearest to the Yosemite Valley, is the Mariposa Grove, some thirty-five miles away. In it there are about 300 big trees, intermingled with many fine firs, pines, and American cedars, insignificant only because of their nearness to the monsters; and after a visitor has measured one tree, walked through another, mounted by a ladder the fallen stump of a third (possibly a good opportunity for a 'stump' oration), and driven, coach and all, through a fourth, he may fairly claim to have made their familiar acquaintance. The largest tree is the 'Grizzly Giant,' 33 feet in diameter from root to root, and 20 feet in diameter at 13 feet from the ground, which is a really fairer estimate, as it preserves this width for quite 100 feet up. The tree through which the road is tunnelled is 30 feet in diameter ; the height of the highest tree is 337 feet.

These enormous fir-trees belong to the species *Sequoia gigantea*, known as *Wellingtonia gigantea* in England. Their wood is reddish ; and their bark a loose, red, fibrous substance, deeply-grooved, and, on at least one tree, fully three feet thick, but their roots never grow very deep. Their age is unknown : they have probably existed many centuries. The elevation of the Mariposa Grove is about 6,500 feet above the sea ; and it is curious that the more southern is the latitude of any of the seven groves, the higher is its elevation above the sea, a fact which seems to show that the trees are very capricious in the choice of their climate.

The railway onwards to San Francisco passes through a desolate plain, occasionally cultivated or used for grazing cattle. Nearer the sea there are hills, after which for some distance the train runs along the bay towards Oakland, where a westward-bound traveller sees the last of American railroads. A twenty minutes' ferry across the harbour brings him to San Francisco.

American car-travelling is certainly comfortable and sumptuous, though painfully dusty, and often very unpunctual in the West; and the sleeping-cars are the best in the world. Everything must, of course, have its disadvantages, and when a screaming baby makes its appearance in a car during the night, it is hardly surprising if the good temper of the other fifty inmates has deserted them by the following morning. There ought to be a special car for squalling babies. Fancy fifty of them together, all privileged to enjoy each other's screams! Little can be said for the civility of American guards or conductors. On the contrary, their rudeness is intolerable, and they evidently wish you to understand that speaking at all is a matter of the greatest condescension: while in fact, they seldom descend from their lofty pedestals unless they have the clearest visions of some substantial bribe. It is a very serious matter that travelling on American railroads undoubtedly involves a greater risk than on railways in any other country. Big or small accidents, to which the American public seem resigned and helpless, are of almost daily occurrence; but they are so strenuously hushed up by the officials, that in England we probably hear of about one-fiftieth of those that really occur. Misplaced economy, arising from monopolies, is their invariable cause;

and weak engines, overloaded trains, unfenced lines or bridges, where cattle may stray at their leisure, and steep gradients are fully sufficient to account for the frequency of the disasters.

The general appearance of San Francisco is very like that of large eastern American towns, but its weather is not always quite so genial as that in many parts of its neighbourhood, for in these the climate is the pleasantest in the world, and the almost perpetual English June brings out a profusion of strawberries, apples, geraniums, fuchsias, heliotrope, veronicas, and all kinds of fruits and flowers, which are seldom out of season throughout the entire year.

San Francisco harbour is an ideal one; a wide land-locked lake, having one narrow outlet through the 'Golden Gate;' but, like the eastern ports, it is singularly unfortified, and every true American now argues in favour of spending the United States surplus upon coast defence; unless, indeed, we can persuade his generosity to assist us in paying off our national debt. At this moment fleets from Chili or Japan could compel San Francisco to capitulate for the asking, though the ultimate consequences to them would of course be very disastrous.

The wide and busy streets are blocked by tram-cars, which are not worked by horses, but attached to and detached from a wire rope, moved along by steam-power in a groove under the road. The rope is even strong enough to draw the cars uphill, and although it requires to be constantly renewed, it is said to be economical, and at any rate does not need to be fed.

Among the largest of the buildings is the Palace Hotel, which is of an overwhelming size, even in comparison with other hotels in America. In that country pre-eminently, the condition of the hotels indicates the success and popularity of the town in which they are built; all Americans are travellers either for business or pleasure, and it is the interest of every rising or ambitious town to provide the very best accommodation.

About three miles from San Francisco is the Cliff House, a favourite excursion-place for tourists, overlooking the curious seal-rock, which has been from time immemorial the metropolis of seals. They lie there in heaps, scuttling along the rock and into the ocean, and even from the shore their barking is very distinctly heard.

But by far the most extraordinary part of the city is Chinatown, which is always visited in the company of a detective. Among the many pig-sties, the most revolting are the lodging-houses and opium-dens; for it is the Chinaman's delight to live and sleep as many as possible in one room;

and although a law exists to prevent it, their
private guilds nullify the law effectually by offering
a reward to any convicted victim. In a chemist's
shop the chief drugs seem to be antler-horns and
root-shavings; jewellers are very industrious with
pure 24-carat gold, and the best Chinese restaurant
is well arranged for European guests. A joss-
house is a ceremonious eccentricity. In a room
of ordinary size at the top of a house, the small
wooden joss or idol sits under a gorgeous canopy
of wood and paper, brilliantly painted, and carved
Chinese fashion. He is guarded by two small
wooden attendants, and presides over an elaborate
altar, fitted with many utensils. Not the least of
these is a tin receptacle for offerings of chicken
and other dainties, which the spirit of the joss
comes down to eat, provided, of course, that he is
not forestalled by his priest; and near the walls
there are spears and other processional emblems,
which are usually carried about the streets at a
funeral, as Chinese funerals are very festive occasions. In concluding with a Chinese theatre,
foreigners, after passing through the green-room,
are each allotted a chair on the side of the stage,
in full view of the audience. This is an especial
privilege of white men, who, notwithstanding this
outward respect in San Francisco, are colloquially
spoken of by the Chinese as 'fang kwai,' or

foreign devils. The performance is a deafening clatter: the so-called orchestra, which sits behind the actors, keeps up a perpetual din of discordant and noisy instruments throughout the entire piece, and, as the play goes on every night from five o'clock till twelve, and there are no scenes and no curtain, the occupation must be excessively exhausting. There are no actresses, women being always personated.

The recent question of the Chinese in Australia has given a peculiar interest to the presence of Chinese in San Francisco. Notwithstanding the constitutional freedom of the United States, a resident Chinaman may never become a citizen, even if he lives there a lifetime; and since the low wages with which they are content seriously interfere with the monopoly of the more expensive American workman, a restrictive law has, till very recently, absolutely prohibited their immigration, if they have not been in the country before. Dissatisfied, however, with this stringency, the Western States have now prevailed upon the President and Congress to pass an act putting a stop to Chinese immigration altogether; and the issue of this deliberate infraction of international comity may still be awaited with no little curiosity. 'We are ruined by Chinese cheap labour: and he went for that heathen Chinee.' In British Columbia the feeling of jealousy is not so rampant, and only a fine of fifty dollars ahead is inflicted.

Some of the enemies of the Chinese declare that they introduce opium-smoking and other vices. But white men prefer tobacco to opium; and it must be reluctantly admitted that in several respects they cannot boast of great superiority, while in others they have different habits and inclinations. The Chinese are dirty; but the filth of their lodging-houses could be perfectly remedied by a more efficient police organisation (as is, in fact, the case in Hong Kong), for what can be expected from two policemen to the whole 40,000 of Chinatown?

Others of their enemies, with irreconcilable contradiction, but with more plausibility, pronounce the habits of the Chinese to be obnoxious because they cannot blend with European customs. If this is honestly the case, that the Chinese are practically a burden upon the life of European colonists, then their enemies' contention assumes an argumentative shape; and it is for the latter to determine at what point the Chinese 'burden' becomes really so insufferable that they have a right to demand redress; whereupon the extent of redress to which they are justly entitled may become a fit matter for diplomatic correspondence.

Many say this severe legislation in America has

been caused by the Irish vote. Possibly this is so; since it has become throughout the States the bane of corrupt politicians, who will oust the Chinese, express such opinions upon foreign questions as may gain them votes, or commit any other enormity, in the hope that it will secure their election.

Chinese ingenuity in reducing the late exclusion law to a dead letter was very remarkable; and as their wives were usually left behind in China, the population would have rapidly diminished if no such scheme had existed. To a Chinaman contemplating for the first time a visit to San Francisco, a letter was sent, describing in detail the city, its streets, its buildings, its tram-fares, and so on. On his arrival he pleaded that he had been there before, but had lost the certificate enabling him to return; a statement unscrupulously corroborated by five or six other Chinamen, who are always ready to swear to the truth of whatever is expedient. When cross-examined through an interpreter, he took care to show an intimate knowledge of the ways of the town, which he had learnt by heart from his private letter of introduction! And who was to gainsay his assertions?

As to our Australian colonies, it seems clear that we must be at least guided by their wishes in so personal a question; but, speaking in the abstract, the exclusion of the Chinaman's cheap work, even if he is in the habit of returning to his own country to spend his accumulated wages, is a blow to industry, and a check upon the trade of the colony. Unless his numbers are so great that they stimulate a revolt, and endanger our sovereignty, which, to judge from the analogy of Singapore and Hong Kong, is most improbable; or unless the country is too poor to support him; or thirdly, as has been suggested, he is a positive plague upon European life, there is no sufficient reason why he should be placed in a different category to every other human being, and condemned to an exile which is simply a punishment for having proved himself too industrious.

Before bidding farewell to America and its exquisite scenery, it is not inappropriate to make a few very brief remarks upon some of its general characteristics. Upon any ordinary visitor to the States, the evils, as well as the good, of an ultra-democratic government are everywhere indelibly impressed. Throughout the country there is a wholesale system of bribery and corruption, especially prominent in politics, which is not even to be compared with our worst days under George III. Individual senators *have* been suspected of giving secret bribes to the legislature; municipalities are a perfect nest of corruption, and only a short time ago a wealthy inhabitant of San Francisco was on his trial for bribing a juror. Mayors, custom-house officers, policemen, must all be staunch adherents of one or other political party, or else must forego every chance of promotion.[1]

In the next place, the so-called independence of the people really fosters the most shameless incivility. No one knows his own position, and, as usual, until it becomes a question of the almighty dollar (whose almightiness is very repulsive in practice), or, be it said to their honour, there is a lady to be provided for, the citizens of the States are often accustomed to treat a stranger with unabashed insolence and contempt. This modern spirit of independence annihilates good manners, fans discontent, and looks upon every position of subservience, however advantageous to all parties, as a kind of ill-defined insult to the dignity of the server. The extreme difficulty of getting servants, and the high rate of labourers' wages which makes

---

[1] During our stay at Niagara, it appeared that the porter of our hotel was an ex-English police sergeant, who had come out to the United States for the purpose of joining their police force. On his arrival he found that, apart from five years' residence in order to qualify as a citizen, he was required to profess himself either a sound Republican, or otherwise an unflinching Democrat, and he announced his immediate intention of returning to England, to re-enlist as a private in the force he had deserted, rather than submit to such despotic conditions.

living at least twice as costly as in England, are effects of the prevalent ideas. The want of courtesy and refinement is particularly flagrant on a railway journey, and is there little calculated to prepossess an unprejudiced spectator. From all such charges the real gentlemen are of course exempt; they are always very amusing, hospitable, and communicative, and their occasional inquisitiveness is but natural to every American, and only strange to European ideas.

But the Americans have also many good qualities. We may well learn a lesson from their indomitable energy, and of their mechanical and inventive genius we may almost stand in awe. In thirty short years who but the Americans would have opened out the whole western continent by railway communication? Who but they would have contrived to ferry a whole train over a river, as happens in crossing the Columbia at Kaláma? Their electric light inventions have been most persevering, and their mining has, on the whole, been very successful; for although bogus mines have increased the risk of investments, the many prizes that have been won have half-atoned for their want of success. In 1867, for seven millions of dollars, the United States bought Alaska from the Russians, to whom that country had been little better than a white elephant. To-day the energy of the Americans has turned the icebergs into most valuable gold-mines, and many of the barren plains into crops of oats and barley. The nation is an eminently practical one; it knows it; and takes advantage of its genius.

CHAPTER III.

JAPAN: THE NEIGHBOURHOOD OF YOKOHAMA AND TOKIO.

WITH but five passengers on board (besides a crowd of Chinese in the steerage), there is something inexpressibly dreary in sailing from San Francisco for Japan; and the prospect of three weeks' enforced idleness at sea is not brightened by the thought of how much could be done in the same time on land. At intervals perhaps a shoal of flying-fish now and then varies the monotony. At meals there is ample opportunity of tasting Californian wines, but the Zinfandel claret, which is stronger and purer than the French wine, is the only one really presentable. It is instructive to elicit from agreeable Germans on board that their national food includes raw salmon, raw herring, raw sardines, raw pork, raw Pomeranian goose, sour cabbage, and spoilt cheese! But beyond a few games there is little to enliven the journey. The inevitable loss of a day is always a distraction. The day is skipped at the midnight before the ship reaches the 180th meridian of longitude, and in our passage that meridian was reached precisely as the clock was pointing to midnight on a Saturday. As there were several missionaries on board, they had the strongest aversion to missing out Sunday, and, accordingly, after much dispute, the captain could only appease them by ordering the following day to be Sunday up till mid-day, and Monday during the afternoon and evening.

After so long an exile from land, it is no slight relief to see the distant snowy gleam of Fuji-yama, the great sacred mountain of Japan, 12,000 feet high, even though the ship may still be a hundred miles from shore. Nor is one's pleasure diminished by at length rejoining the world at Yokohama, after having endured a nearly three weeks' passage, and travelled between four and five thousand miles. During the voyage there is scarcely to be seen a single fish, very seldom a ship, and never a trace of land, and its only consolation is that the vacancy produced in one's mind is an excellent preparative for receiving vivid impressions of Japan. A steam launch awaits the mail-steamer passengers, for the harbour is merely a roadstead, and lands them at the custom-house; after which the race in jin-rikishas along the road by the sea to the excellent European 'Grand Hotel' is quite as exciting as an Ascot finish. Each jin-rikisha usually holds one person; it has some resemblance both to a pony-chaise and a wheelbarrow, and is drawn by a trotting man.

To find oneself landed in Japan, 10,000 miles from home, in a country probably accessible but once in a lifetime, is so fanciful a reality that at first it seems more like a tantalising dream. The streets of Yokohama, lined with long rows of Japanese houses, generally but one storey high, are adorned with Japanese or even English advertisements; groups of demure and smiling people still walk about in their neat native dress of dark-blue cotton; women and children carry babies on their backs; and a few artistic curiosities peep here and there from the corners of the shops. It is usually the fashion among the women, so soon as they are married, to disfigure themselves as far as possible by blackening their teeth. The custom is a most singular one; for although European imagination is much apt to exaggerate their beauty, who can tell the charms of which these amiable guys have been thus deprived? At evening the streets afford many lively attractions. Among public amusements juggling and blinded wrestlers are very popular; but the theatres also draw large audiences. The plays are an improvement upon a Chinese performance, for they make use of a curtain, occasionally a caricature of scenery, and a less deafening, though not more musical, orchestra. But the actors have sometimes an odd propensity of appearing and vanishing along a side arm of the stage which runs far back into the pit.

Two miles round a bay from Yokohama is the little village of Kanagáwa, at one time a competitor for the commercial position now gained by the better known town. It was actually opened as a treaty-port on July 1, 1859, but merchants insisted upon the superiority of Yokohama, and ministers and consuls have tacitly acquiesced in their view.[1]

We cannot quite overlook the history of Japan. Of much of it there is no record whatever, but a very brief summary of what remains, even at the risk of tediousness, must be excused as necessary in order to appreciate the places to be visited. Since about B.C. 660 there have been 123 mikados without a single change of dynasty; the first being a certain Jimmu, and the last the present Emperor Mutsuhito. Their court formerly resided at Kioto. Yoritomo (A.D 1192-1199), a great general and statesman, was the first to create the dual system of government—government by two emperors—which continued without intermission till 1868. He assumed the title of Shôgun,

[1] See p. 59 *inf.* note 2.

(commander-in-chief) or Tycoon (Tai-kun, 'great prince'), sometimes known as secular emperor, took Kamakura for his capital, and thenceforward reduced the Mikado, or spiritual emperor, to the condition of a mere imprisoned idol, a glance at whose dazzling countenance was of course reputed to cause instant blindness. During the generalship of Yoritomo, and the rule of his successors, the *daimiós*, or feudal lords, gradually drew around them their *samurai* or vassals, and their retainers; and acquired their lands. In A.D. 1603–4 Iye-ásu, often inaccurately called the first shôgun, set himself up to be a very powerful ruler. He perfected the duarchy and feudal system of government, and founded the city of Yeddo. In the reign of Iye-mitsu (1623–1649), the third shôgun, also a powerful ruler, there took place a fierce persecution of the Christian inhabitants of the country; and from about 1637 to 1853 the history of Japan is a complete blank, all Europeans but the Dutch being excluded; and even they being only allowed to touch at the small island of Déshima, near the port of Nagasaki, for purposes of commerce. In the latter year Commodore Perry appeared, with an expedition from the United States, and effected a primitive treaty in 1854, while in 1858 Lord Elgin signed the treaty of Yeddo for England. The present Mikado,

Mutsuhito, was a child when he began his reign on Feb. 3, 1867, and was therefore only a figurehead in the great revolution of 1868-70, which no doubt had been brewing for some considerable time. It recalled the Mikado from his hereditary confinement, established his power, set alight the blaze of reform, and annihilated the Tycoon, who happened at that crisis to be an unpopular man, and he retired from that moment into private life. The daimiôs at first sided with the Mikado against the Tycoon: but subsequently the Mikado, by some most inexplicable intrigue, and probably the favour of public opinion, was strong enough to turn round upon the daimiôs, who appear to have become a very degenerate race, and to seize their lands, without the slightest resistance, for the benefit of the government. Some little compensation was given them. The name of Yeddo was then changed to Tokio, and it supplanted Kioto as the capital of the empire. In 1877 the rebellion of the Satsuma clan, led by Saigo, commander-in-chief of the army, was a far more terrible civil war than the revolution of 1868; and it has been the most dangerous uprising with which the reigning Mikado's government has ever had to deal. The country is now governed by the Mikado, assisted by his ministers, who resemble our cabinet, except that they are not at present trammelled by any obstructive representative institutions. They perform their duties well.[1]

The present intercourse of the Japanese with European nations is regulated by treaties of which the earliest, already mentioned, was that concluded with the United States in 1854. Every European with whose nation a treaty has been signed, and every citizen of the United States, now enjoys the right of exterritoriality; that is, no Japanese court has jurisdiction over him. The Japanese have never ceased to regret this concession, and meanwhile refuse to open out their country to Europeans not provided with passports till the treaties have been revised, and this restriction withdrawn.[2] Europeans, on their part, will not agree to this proposal till the Japanese can show that their code of law is properly administered, and is consistent with Western principles. Japan, as a preliminary step, has therefore already revised her criminal code with able foreign assistance, while her civil code is now in course of revision, although it will

---

[1] The revenue of Japan is very nearly balanced by its expenditure in 1886-7 there was only a small surplus of about 1,000*l*. Of this revenue the land tax yields about 7,000,000*l*., and the tax on *saké* (rice-beer and spirit) about 2,000,000*l*.; together nearly four-fifths of the whole.

[2] Passports are, however, not required by travellers in the six ports mentioned in the treaties, viz., Kanagáwa (Yokohama), Nagasaki, Hakodate, Niigata, Hiogo (Kobé), Osaka, nor within a radius of ten ' *ri* ' from each—nearly 24½ miles.

probably not be finished for at least another year. The Code Napoléon is being extensively followed. It has also been suggested that the Japanese government should in part appoint a foreign judiciary, but European nations have tended to be unfairly exacting in their proposals, and it is but reasonable to expect that they should moderate their demands.

But digressions upon Japanese history and politics are growing interminable, and it is fully time to take jin-rikishas to the railway-station at Yokohama, and start by train for Tokio. What neat and comfortable little carriages, and what a relief to be free from the baby-screams of American cars! There and everywhere Japanese inscriptions are posted up side by side with English translations—so hastily are the Japanese becoming Europeanised; the names of the stations are transcribed into English; and there are even English injunctions about passengers not crossing the line. In fact, English has been adopted as the official foreign language. By the edge of the railway are many swamps of irrigated rice-fields; but though the labourers earn only about 8$d.$ a day, the large consumption of manure makes the crop, in comparison, a costly one.

Tokio is reached in about fifty minutes. The general look of the streets is not very dissimilar to that of Yokohama, but the city extends over an immense area, and has a population of no less than 1,300,000. Its temples of Shiba are inferior only to those at Nikko, shortly to be described. Their elaborate gold lacquer-work,[1] massive gilt pillars, gilt lotus-flowers, and panels of carving in deep relief are particularly remarkable; their tall and quaint stone-lanterns, presented by ancient daimiôs, and arrayed in grim rows at the side of the courtyards, are peculiar to most of the larger temples in Japan.

The Mikado's private gardens, of which his Majesty owns several in different parts of the town, are all models of the tidy industry of Japanese culture. They are in every way artificial; the mounds, banks, ponds, and rockeries are all made; and even large trees have been successfully transplanted into the newly-risen garden landscapes. In the Rikiu gardens are the imperial preserves and decoys of wild duck. The birds are very dexterously caught with a net, as they fly out of a ditch, by a keeper who has concealed himself behind a bush; but the operation can only be seen by the special permission of their imperial master, and this is presumably withheld unless they are required for the imperial table.

[1] Lacquer is obtained from a gum or resin extracted out of the lacquer-tree.

The magnificent new palace of the Mikado in Tokio is still incomplete. Like almost all strictly Japanese houses, it has but a ground floor, but it is made formidable by the protection of three lines of fortification and two moats. The work in the interior is very beautiful. The ceilings are mostly constructed of red or black lacquered crossbeams, usually enclosing panels of the peculiar Japanese paper, designed in very tasteful patterns, but sometimes, instead, the panels are of silk, skilfully interwoven with flowers. On the walls also are hung exquisite pieces of interwoven silk, and the wooden floors are very carefully inlaid; besides which the great reception and dining rooms are shut off from the passage by a lacquered wooden framework of open panels, whose handsome symmetry much enhances the general effect. In the labyrinth of private rooms, including the Mikado's and Empress's intended bedrooms, the ornamentation is in a somewhat different style, the rooms are smaller, and the floors are covered with the Japanese *tatámé* matting, whose neatness, whiteness, and softness alike make it very inviting to walk on. Every piece of matting is exactly the same size, about 6 feet by 4 feet, and $1\frac{1}{2}$ inches thick, and as no one ever dreams of fitting the matting to the rooms, all Japanese rooms have to be built to take in so many pieces of matting.

As to its architecture, the palace is well-proportioned. It is everywhere profusely decorated with the imperial crest of a chrysanthemum of sixteen petals, and the beauty of the wood throughout is that it is not marred by a single knot, nor is it anywhere painted, waxed, or varnished.

Many Japanese gentlemen in Tokio belong to the charming little Koyo-kwan or Maple Club—a real Japanese club—whose entertainments of professional dancing are occasionally patronised by royalty, which makes it a favourite rendezvous of Japanese society. The maples around it, from which it takes its name, are in autumn a most exquisite crimson. It has no library and no writing-room—perhaps such Europeanisms would have spoilt its native appearance; and the delightful matting seems to dispense with any need of furniture. The floor of the dining-room is laid out, near the sliding-screen walls, with two rows of square cushions, on which the members sit cross-legged, to eat their dinners with chopsticks from the small black trays put before them. Before leaving, every visitor is offered a dish of sugar-plums made of rice and sugar, and tiny cups of Japanese tea, the usual tokens of Japanese hospitality; after which he is honoured at the door with the lowest of bows from the smiling young waitresses, who have been all along the essence of politeness and attention.

Among the many interesting scenes in Tokio, the Museum contains curious relics of old Japan, including the former head-dress and carriages of the mikados, and the ancient armour of the daimiôs.

Of national pastimes, wrestling-matches are, perhaps, the most popular. The combatants in them are lustily encouraged by the noisy eloquence of their umpire, and weight seems to be the chief element of victory. Innocent race-meetings also meet with the lively approval of the present sovereign; indeed, they are among the few special occasions when he shows himself in public. But, fortunately for his people, they are still unadulterated with the spurious accompaniments of a civilised turf, and its pretexts for betting and scandal.

'He who has not seen Nikko, has not seen what is really beautiful.' So runs the Japanese dogma concerning the finest temples in Japan. They are about eighty miles from Tokio, sixty by rail to Utsunomiya, through a country prettily wooded, and covered with small fields of rice, wheat, barley, tea, and cotton, and sometimes plantations of bamboo; and then twenty miles on, by a road in itself quite worthy of the excursion.

Jin-rikishas are the proper mode of conveyance, each being drawn for this journey by two men, whose trotting powers in the long run would win a race with a carriage, although the same men go the whole distance, and their strict fare is $1\frac{1}{2}d$. a mile! Along the whole length of this capital road to Nikko has been planted a more or less continuous avenue of firs and cryptomerias, surrounded by scenery not unlike a pretty English pheasant covert, though of course the dark red maple has no English equal. Here and there it is intersected by a village, characteristically neat and clean, where national custom lays down that the babies' hair shall be shaved entirely off, or else only left as a small circular top-knot at the back of their heads. Twice in the twenty miles the jin-rikisha-men stop at an inn to refresh themselves with rice and soup, and instantly a traveller's party is attended to by the smiling little inn-girls, who bring out tea, and waddle and bow most amiably, as they shuffle along in their clumsy shoes. Occasionally a horse passes by, the very best of which (and they are not inferior horses) can be bought for two guineas, as their work is in little demand; for when, by chance, men themselves do not do duty as beasts of burden, their place is supplied by a breed of oxen, so small that they must be very distantly related to their connections in Europe. By far the most wonderful part of the journey, however, begins about ten miles from Nikko, when a continuation of the magnificent avenue of cryptomerias, here quite 100 feet high, overshadows the road almost without a break until the traveller reaches his destination at the Nikko hotel.

This hotel is one of those in Japan whose proprietor has not become infected with the European mania, and as it still retains some signs of primitiveness, one of its bedrooms is entitled to some description. It has a real door into the passage, but one of its walls consists of four screens which slide like folding-doors—quite a common arrangement—similar to the walls in the native club at Tokio; by which means an inmate of the hotel can walk through the wall at any point he pleases, and thus intrude upon his neighbour's abode. Another side is a wooden lattice-work of running screens covered with rice-paper, the latter being the almost universal substitute for glass windows. The floor is laid out with tatámé matting, and although there is a tolerable bedstead instead of quilts on the ground, this is a European innovation altogether out of keeping with the rest of the house. A small portable charcoal fire is the only means of keeping warm in winter (other fires are not Japanese); and though the frost is not without its effect upon the temperature of so slender an apartment, it yet allows some chance of avoiding a sleepless night. A Japanese room contains no furniture, unless it is a small low table: the list in these bedrooms of one table and one chair is exceptionally large.

A mountain torrent, spanned by two bridges a few yards apart, separates the village from the temples at Nikko. The lower one is for mankind in general, the upper is a sacred red-lacquered bridge, which may only be crossed by the Mikado and the chief priest.

The two great religions of Japan are Shintoism and Buddhism, but their doctrines and traditions are too complicated to be deserving of careful inquiry. Very briefly, Shintoism (from the Chinese word Shin-tô, 'Way of the Gods') is primarily ancestor-worship, and has some slight similarity to the Anglo-Saxon adoration of Wodin and Thor. Buddhism, on the other hand, with its belief in signs and saints, may be conceived, in this particular respect, to have a faint resemblance to Roman Catholicism. The religions are not antagonistic, and have developed side by side, though not without important effects upon each other. Shintoism is the original national religion of Japan, and merely requires its adherents to follow their own impulses as to what is right, and to obey the laws of the State. It has no bible. Buddhism was preached in Japan by Chinese monks in A.D. 623 (*i.e.*, about twelve hundred years after Prince Siddhârtha or Buddha), and was firmly rooted there in A.D. 800. In the thirteenth century various 'heresies,' if the term may be used, crept over from China, but it remained, notwithstanding, the prevalent religion of the country. Its chief doctrine is the transmigration of the soul, which is always supposed to be on the way to Nirvâna, or eternal rest; but the number of transmigrations before it attains this goal depends upon the uprightness and self-control of each of its individual possessors. In the revolution of 1868 many Buddhist temples became Shinto ones, and Shintoism was again restored as the established State religion.

The Nikko temples are the companions of magnificent groves of cryptomerias. The most important temple is the great red and gilt one built of wood by the famous shôgun Iye-ásu (A.D. 1603), formerly a Buddhist edifice, but changed in 1868 to the government religion of Shintoism. Near a tall, five-storied pagoda, its grounds are entered under a fine stone *torii*, or sacred archway, always indicative of a Shinto as opposed to a Buddhist temple, and inside, the rows of curious stone lanterns, which abound in

Torii and Pagoda at the Entrance to the Shinto Temple, Nikko

all the Nikko temples, were the gifts of powerful daimiôs. Not far from these is the stable of the god's horse, ornamented by celebrated carvings of monkeys; but as the horse itself is always reserved for its master, it has been condemned to make eating the sole object of its life. Just beyond, under an elaborate roof is a cistern of solid granite, so accurately balanced that the water flows out over all its edges at once, and at the foot of a flight of steps (where a Japanese inscription commands even a royal prince to dismount from his horse before ascending, though no animal short of a Pegasus would be likely to attempt the feat), visitors are sometimes received by the Shinto priests, attired in their full robes of purple or pale green, with a light gauze head-dress. They are then conducted up the steps, past a pagoda, a large bronze bell, and a bronze candelabrum given to an earlier shôgun by the Dutch traders. The main temple is approached through a carved and lacquered gateway, guarded by two dragon-like lions, which are symbols of Shintoism; but no one may go in till his boots have been removed—out of respect (it appears) for the matting, not the god. This gorgeous oriental building, like other Shinto temples, consists of three or four rooms; in the first of which a mirror, a drum, and some ribbon-like strips of paper are the special characteristics of the Shinto god. At Nikko this chamber also contains some small, well-designed pillars of pure gilt lacquer, of a composition so solid, peculiar, and costly that they are probably unknown elsewhere in Japan. An anteroom leads to the second chamber, into which it is always a privilege to enter. It is about five and twenty feet long by ten wide, its ceiling is adorned with narrow lacquered crossbeams enclosing artistically painted panels, and its walls are decorated with intricate carvings. Two or three boxes on the floor encase the armour of an early shôgun, in appearance very similar to English armour in the time of Cromwell; and by its side are three valuable swords, one of which has been presented by the reigning Mikado. In the third chamber at the back is the shrine of the god, who is probably represented by a mirror. It is closed to ordinary mortals, and its seclusion may only be disturbed by the Mikado and the head priest. Over an archway in the court-yard is a celebrated wooden carving of a sleeping cat, who, like its famous Cheshire contemporary in *Alice's Adventures in Wonderland*, grins good-naturedly at all comers; and in a separate part of the temple, a small offering will generally induce a white-robed priest to perform the mournful dance with which the god is humoured every morning. The massive bronze tomb of Iye-ásu is ornamented with bronze

Outer Archway to Shrine of Shinto Temple, Nikko

lotus-flowers and storks, and the latter are especially respected as the emblems of good luck.

The second temple is still dedicated to Buddha, and was built by the celebrated shôgun Iye-mitsu (A.D. 1623-1649). Here the gateways are guarded by hideous scowling giants, painted red and green, who, like the Shinto lions, are entrusted with the responsibility of terrifying evil spirits. The main temple contains three rooms; the carving is perhaps slightly better than that in the temple of Iye-asu, and there is more gilt decoration. A view of the inner room is again a matter of privilege; it is quite dark and shut in, lighted only by a few Japanese lanterns. At the back stands a cabinet in which the Buddha is enclosed; outside it he is attended by two or three images; while the whole room is thickly gilt and lacquered, and handsomely decorated by four gilt pillars and a small central canopy of gilt spangles. Under this the head priest only is allowed to sit. The Buddhist bible, kept in the temple, is written on illuminated silk scrolls; and it is noticeable that the Buddhist priests differ from the Shinto ones in wearing no head-dress, and being completely shorn. On leaving the temple the tomb of Iye-mitsu is close at hand.

The pillar called Sorinto, dating from 1643, is erected near the temples. It is a black copper cylinder, flowering at the top into six lotus-shaped cups, from each of which hang small brass bells. The Buddhist temple of Rinnôji is also near, and is picturesquely situated in front of a neat tea-garden and (in winter) showy chrysanthemums.

Among the most agreeable of the expeditions to be made from Nikko, is that up the mountains to Chiusenji Lake. The climb, however, is rather steep, and each traveller is therefore half-expected to encourage local industry by submitting to being taken up in a *kago*. This kind of carriage is a form of bamboo basket, slung upon a pole, and lifted by one or two men at each end. Its occupant sits cross-legged, and tries to roll himself up into the shape and stolidity of a porcupine; but of course, poor being! all his attempts at comfort are perfectly futile, and he very soon prefers to walk; from which posture he can far better enjoy the pretty mountain scenery and noisy torrents, and the rhododendrons and tall cryptomerias which relieve them.

Yokohama makes capital head-quarters for all these tours inland. Another very pleasant one is to go by rail and jin-rikishas to Miyanóshīta and Atámi. After leaving the railway at Kodzu, the small thatched cottages, with their torn rice-paper windows, seem wild and rustic as compared with the more frequented regions of Nikko, and towards the end of November the few lingering chrysanthemums in their gardens have begun to droop and fade; but the roads are excellent, and the mountains and valleys are none the less engaging for the frequent prominence of the red maples and evergreen bamboos. Beyond Miyanóshita there are quantities of *káya*, a species of small pampas-grass, and in the neighbourhood the number of fuming geysers and fine sulphur springs indicates very clearly the volcanic nature of the country. At one place there is a large stone image of Jizo, the patron god of travellers, near which his lesser likenesses adorn the pathway at regular intervals, and announce to each wayfarer the completion of another *cho* (120 yards). Soon this path turns into the old 'Tokaido' road from Tokio to Kioto, and leads close past the gates of the Mikado's new palace at Hakóné. This building commands a fine view of the pretty Hakóné lake and mountains, and is built in French chateau style, as his Majesty has a great liking for European fashions; but a Japanese wing has also been added, at the particular request of the Empress. In the European portion the beautiful silk tablecloths, chairs, and curtains are all of native manufacture; the native part is as clean and tidy as usual. Continuing the journey towards Atámi, the succession of natural pictures perhaps reaches its climax at the top of Higáne-san. The beauty of the surrounding ranges, in several places melting away into the sea, is here only dwarfed by the all-absorbing grace of Fuji-san or Fuji-yama, of whose magnificent snowy cone and glorious majestic sweep the Japanese have good reason to be proud.[1] It is about 12,000 feet high; and, though once an active volcano, it has shown no signs of activity since 1707. From Higáne-san the descent to Atámi is a steep one, and in the dim distance across the ocean the ceaseless smoke of the volcanic island of Oshima is constantly curling up out of the waves. The village of Atámi is situated by a cove of the sea, and is celebrated for the baths from its hot salt-water geyser.

The twenty miles' jin-rikisha ride from Atámi back to the railway at Kodzu lies by the coast; and the varied irregularities of the mountains form a continuous and most enchanting contrast to the soft deep blue of the sea; while, in the villages, the cottage-gardens in autumn are studded with orange-trees, and ripe with golden fruit.

On the coast, about three miles from one of

[1] Pictures of Fuji-yama are constantly worked upon their screens and silks.

the railway stations, is the island of Enoshima, noted for its native and imported shells, and separated from the mainland by a sandy promontory, which must be crossed at high tide in a Japanese punt between two lines of surf. At high tide, too, the exploration of its long and dismal cave is a somewhat precarious adventure, and there is nothing to see in it after all but a small shrine.

A few miles eastward, near Kamakura, is the giant 'Dai-butsu,' or idol of Great Buddha. The history of this venerable seated being, who sits almost 50 feet high, and has a width from ear to ear of no less than $17\frac{3}{4}$ feet, is wrapt in obscurity; but he was probably cast in A.D. 1252, and is made of separate sheets of bronze, brazed together and chiselled off on the outside. His proportions are perfect; and his benignant look is remarkably expressive of the intellectual calm in which Buddha is believed to rest. Before him are two large bronze lotus-plants, and two brazen lanterns; inside him is a chapel, several smaller gilt Buddhas, and numerous paper relics, the gifts of devout pilgrims. He is exposed to all weathers.

Kamakura itself is proud of a famous Shinto temple of the god of war, founded by the powerful Yoritomo and his ancestor Yori-yoshi about the twelfth century. Like many others, it contains respected curiosities; but even the most respected temples are apt to grow monotonous. It is something like journeying through all the parish churches in England. The road between Kamakura and Yokohama leads mainly through small fields, very characteristic of Japanese agriculture, and low precipitous hills, all gaily scattered with indigenous trees.

CHAPTER IV.

JAPAN: KOBÉ TO KIOTO AND NAGASAKI.

WITH the help of one of the English-built coasting steamers, it is easy to shift one's head-quarters from Yokohama to the more southern port of Kobé. By no means the least interesting part of it is the city prison, to which strangers are only admitted through the kindness of the provincial prefect or governor; and as his European carriage is the only vehicle of its kind in the district, it creates quite a sensation should he lend it them to drive through the streets. Even its coachman is in European livery. The prisoners' cells are arranged round courtyards, and each cell, which is enclosed by thick wooden bars so as to secure ample ventilation, measures about 20 ft. by 15, and can contain about seventeen prisoners. They are therefore able to talk at night; and, as all the prisoners locked up in the same cell have been guilty of the same misdemeanour, they have perhaps a dangerous fellow-feeling which might instigate plots for escape. The prisoners' dress is a light red cotton, and their labour, though not very hard, is useful, the men making mostly matches and the women shoes of straw. As the governor's inspecting party approach, their heads all respectfully crouch to the ground. Their food generally consists of hot water and three parts of wheat to one of rice; but since the national food is little else than rice, fish, and weak tea, it must be a difficult task to make the prison diet very distasteful. A special cell is set apart for sick women. Altogether the prison appears very clean and well-managed, and its condition bears trustworthy evidence to the progress of civilisation in Japan.

Osaka is an hour and a quarter by train from Kobé. Of its ancient castle, 360 years old, the fortified walls of gigantic stones alone remain, a triumph of Japanese energy before the invention of modern machines, the new buildings inside being used as soldiers' barracks. But the city is chiefly important for its mechanical manufactures, and its tall chimneys and black smoke are rudely suggestive of an incipient Birmingham or Sheffield. The Japanese Mint and Arsenal have been erected here, closely modelled upon the most improved European originals, and although some European superintendents are still employed by their authorities, they are, like European captains in the Japanese navy, being gradually ousted as the natives learn their work. There are, for instance, one or two English chemists employed as assayers to the Mint, and an Italian major directs the Arsenal, their salaries being fixed on a much higher scale than that of ordinary Japanese officials.[1] The leading bank in Osaka is, however, quite Japanese, and its unassuming dinginess cannot pretend to vie with the magnificence of our palatial counting-houses.

On the outskirts of Osaka, the temple of Tennôji presents a fine old pagoda, five storeys high, and ornamented with fantastic elephants' heads, and a quaintly carved cloud pattern; but it is far too weather-beaten to display with effect its faded gorgeousness of green and purple. Its exposed paintings are twelve hundred years old. Near one of the gates a smaller temple encloses a bell, which is rung to induce the saintly founder—an illustrious prince, Shôtôku Taishi—to lead the dead to paradise, and the whole shrine is deluged with offerings of dolls and other toys. Close by, in another building, fortune-telling is almost daily in vogue. Each pious suppliant draws from a box a numbered lot, corresponding to the number of a printed fortune with which he is at once provided. This

---

[1] European employés in Japan receive from 1,000*l*. to 3,000*l*. a year. The salary of the Japanese prime minister is 1,600*l*. a year; other principal ministers, and Japanese admirals and generals, receive about 1,000*l*.

document prophesies his future career, no doubt in accordance with the purest tenets of Buddhism; but if he is dissatisfied with it, there is apparently no rule against his drawing again. The method is an ingenious one for suiting every man to his taste.

As there is no railway, the thirty-three miles from Osaka to Nara are best accomplished in jinrikishas, and the monastery of Ho-riu-ji, the oldest Buddhist temple in Japan, makes a convenient half-way halt. It covers a large extent of ground, and, previously to the revolution of 1868, owned no inconsiderable property; but it was then disendowed, and has since been inevitably left to natural decay. Two of its rooms are remarkable. One, containing a large gilt image of Buddha, is hung with swords and mirrors, presented by devout worshippers, men and women, with the notion that these are the articles of the greatest value to their respective sexes. The other, in which are bronze images, has its walls painted with frescoes, and is believed to be twelve centuries old. The paintings are very curious and well-executed; there are no others like them in the country, and they are conjectured to be the work of a Korean artist. The monastery is full of other strange treasures, among which the supposed pupil of Buddha's left eye holds a foremost place.

Nara was the capital of Japan from A.D. 709 to 784. It excels in existing or ruined temples. One of them is environed by splendid trees and cryptomerias, and endless rows of stone lanterns, which are lighted up towards dusk so far as the temple revenues will permit. A second temple contains another Great Buddha, uglier but higher than the idol at Kamakura, and sheltered under a prodigious roof. Here, also, there belongs a very fine bronze bell, of the handsome type and deep tone so common in Japan, which is rung every day by swinging against it a long pole from the outside. An ancient pagoda represents a third temple.

But the crucial moment at Nara is the time spent in lodging at the Musashino inn. With the exception of a carpet, one or two chairs, and a table, and a few glass panes in windows which are otherwise paper, there is nothing in it that is European. At evening an ordinary Japanese dinner is served up, chopsticks and all: a lively experience to look back to, but one which very soon relegates its victim to a meal off toast and eggs. It is brought up on a small square tray in four little dishes, of which two are very uninviting raw fish, one a tasteless boiled fish with a little water to do duty as sauce, and the fourth a bowl of rice. Needless to add, few people would venture upon numbers one and two. Number three could only be acceptable at the point of starvation, and the bowl of rice is spoilt by being boiled in water. During the meal, the Japanese drink their favourite rice-spirit, or *saké*, but after one or two sips a foreigner has no desire to try it again. Afterwards they have a cup of tea.

Japanese food also includes chicken, decayed vegetables, sugar-plums of rice and sugar, and a fruit called persimmon, which has a mixed resemblance to apricots and oranges. The native oranges are very good, and very like tangerines; the strawberries are said to be excellent; but the apples and pears are extremely hard, and only good for cooking. The Japanese never, as a rule, eat butcher's meat, though beef-steak has been lately introduced; and they never have milk, butter, cheese, or bread, the wheat and barley that they grow being used for mixing with the rice. Perhaps their somewhat stunted growth may be accounted for by the want of milk.

The beds in the Nara inn are quite Japanese. Each one is laid out upon the floor, and requires but four comfortable quilts; one is rolled up as a pillow, another serves as a mattress, and two more supply the place of blankets.

Jin-rikisha men can accomplish the thirty miles between Nara and Kioto in about five hours, and the land, especially round Uji, is a prosperous

Sketch in a Japanese Village

tea-district, rich in plantations of tea. In the suburbs of Kioto there is another Great Buddha, this time merely a ponderous head and shoulders, but his ugliness must require much propitiating. The court-yard is enriched by a magnificent bronze bell, very similar to that at Nara, nearly 14 feet high, 9 inches thick, 9 feet in diameter, and weighing over 63 tons.

Kioto is a town full of temples. In the Nishi (or western) Hon-gwan-ji, the running wall-screens of the back rooms are painted with skilful devices by Kano, a celebrated Japanese artist of the seventeenth century, and its *hondo*, or principal hall of worship, is very fine. The Rokakudo (Buddhist) temple is quaint, on account of its peculiar six-sided shape. But a year ago the Higashi (or eastern) Hon-gwan-ji was primed with wonders. It has been three times destroyed by fire, and is being erected for the fourth time, at a cost of some 870,000*l*. It is a colossal structure, and promises to be one of the finest of its kind; but the fact that the disestablished Buddhists have been able to subscribe this large sum in ten years (and the sum is especially large for Japan) goes far, both to prove their devotion, and also to show that there is at least some wealth in the country. Another most astonishing sign of devotion was in readiness to be employed in the work. Hanging from a temporary beam were forty ropes of women's hair, the largest of which had actually been twisted up by the personal sacrifice of 4,000 women, and must have measured some six inches in diameter. Such religious infatuation seems to us almost incredible, and Buddhism is evidently not waning for want of earnest support. The massive wooden pillars of the building are very striking, and in an adjoining outhouse, workmen were then engaged in carving huge trunks in open relief, destined for the capitals of the pillars. The designs, including animals, birds, and flowers, are marvellously executed, and give no uncertain proof of the very artistic talent of the Japanese.

The ancient palaces of the Mikado and Shôgun in Kioto are shown by special order. In the former the most historical feature (and there is little else of interest) is the big hall and its plain wooden pillars, in which, about twenty-five years ago, a Mikado for the first time ever condescended to give an audience to foreigners. The Mikado was the present sovereign's father, and the British Minister, Sir Harry Parkes, was one of the favoured strangers. In the centre of the room is the imperial throne. It is a chair placed under a small square canopy, which is hung all round with white silk, interwoven with stripes of red and black. The floor is the usual tatámé matting, and the whole throne is slightly raised up from it on a framework of black-lacquered wood. Otherwise the hall is unfurnished. The Shôgun's palace is far superior. Its ceilings of black-lacquered cross-beams and designed paper-panels call to mind the yet more perfect ceilings of the Mikado's new palace at Tokio; and its walls of running screens were handsomely painted and gilt by Kano, at the time that the palace was built.

Of all the larger Japanese towns, perhaps Kioto is the most fascinating. Its situation is pretty; its shops neat: its streets are clean, compact, and business-like; and its entire native character is thoroughly genuine. It carries on a very profitable trade in silks and porcelain, and one or two of its manufacturers turn out bronze articles of a very high class, inlaid with gold and silver. But throughout the East very few fancy goods are on view in the shops; all are made to order, and must be bought by a process of bargaining quite consonant with oriental indolence and waste of time. Nor are there any great firms or factories; every man's business is carried on at his own private risk.

Among the expeditions from Kioto are those to Lake Biwa and the Katsura-gawa rapids. The latter is especially charming. After a jin-rikisha ride of thirteen miles to Yamamoto, through woods interspersed with wild camellias, the jin-rikishas and their occupants all embark in a kind of large punt, guided with bamboo poles and short, rough sculls, and thus cleverly floated down the rapids for eight or ten miles. At places the rocky channels require very careful steering, as the punt is being carried away in the rushing stream, hastening round the curves, and gliding past the steep mountain sides, in their trimmings of fir, Spanish chestnut, dwarf bamboo, or wild azaleas. The journey ends at Arashi-yama, whose mountainous banks are resplendent every May with blossoms of wild cherry trees.

In the return from Kioto to Kobé, the railway passes through Osaka; and, embarking again at Kobé for Nagasaki, half the thirty-six hours' passage is spent among the pretty hilly islets of the inland sea, which flows between the middle and southern islands of Japan.[1] The inland sea terminates with the Straits of Shimonoseki, a picturesque outlet, which was the scene, some five-

---

[1] Japan (Nip-pón, 'Sun-land') comprises four main islands The northern one, Yesso, is very cold and snowy, in comparison with other countries in the same latitude. It is partially inhabited by the curious hairy families of Ainôs, who are quite a different race from the other Japanese, and have been the origin of many fables and traditions. The middle island, Hondo (sometimes erroneously called Nip-pon, which is only the name for the whole of Japan), is the largest and most prosperous of the four; the names of the two southern ones are Shikoku and Kiushiu.

and-twenty years ago, of one of the earliest attacks directed by Japanese from their ships and shore batteries upon passing European vessels. Here the narrow waterway is half blocked by numberless fishermen's junks, fitted with primeval sails. They are made of long thin strips, loosely fastened together, so as to be capable of being quickly detached; and sail is shortened by detaching just so many strips as the occasion may require.

The snug little harbour of Nagasaki is one of the most sheltered in the world, and affords an invaluable retreat from the fury of a typhoon. At its entrance is Papenburg Island, the Tarpeian rock of Japan, from which, in 1637, many thousands of Christians are said to have been hurled; and just out at sea Deshima Island has become historical as the place where the Dutch, alone of Europeans, carried on a trade from the seventeenth to the nineteenth centuries.[1]

With the assistance of the autumn monsoon the journey between Nagasaki and Hong Kong takes about three days and a half. Toiling down against it in the spring is a struggle which lasts another day more, and in any case the sea in the Formosa Channel is nearly always rough.

But to bid farewell to Japan is a very painful necessity. Nothing can be more delightful to a

[1] See p. 57 *ante*.

passing traveller, during a short visit in the country, than the amiability and courtesy of all its people. They seem never discontented, never out of temper with each other; always cheerful, always well-met; and they are overwhelmingly civil to a stranger. Good manners are a pleasure to them; their hospitality, alike to friends and foreigners, is the most exemplary and painstaking; and the lesson their manners teach us is surely not one to be lost. For our utilitarian and practical atmosphere seems often so absorbed in business, that we are half accustomed to cast aside civility as an idle formality, and to think it a mere conventional bore.

In their habits the Japanese are extremely cleanly; no people in the world is more fond of its baths, although most of us might not appreciate their very high temperature. Their cleanliness is a great contrast to the dirt of the Chinese, and our inveterate tendency to classify the two nations together is very misleading. They differ in almost every respect. The Japanese are now thirsting for progress, and are keenly sensitive to foreign criticism. The Chinese remain obstinately backward; a railway which their Government sanctioned, in an incautious moment, has since been taken up. The Japanese are exceedingly amiable: the Chinese are cruel, cold, and sullen, and have a deeply-rooted hatred of strangers. The beauty of Japanese ladies is perhaps exaggerated; as a rule they just miss being pretty: but it would indeed be ludicrous to hunt for an Aphrodite throughout the length and breadth of China.

Every year the Japanese are becoming more Europeanised, and from this point of view every visitor to Japan has an advantage over those who tread in his footsteps. Their European fever may be a matter for selfish regret (it is melancholy to watch their renunciation of all their charming customs!), and it has unfortunately been a source of wealth to the 'smartness' of our transatlantic friends and other unscrupulous foreigners; but it is surely very greatly to their credit. It is no easy task for a nation to pocket its national pride, and to admit, before all the nations of the West, that its civilisation is inferior to theirs. Nor have the Japanese pursued their innovations in merely one direction. Politically, they have freed themselves from an absolute despotism, and introduced a kind of dependable oligarchy; soon, it is promised—though we may be doubtful with what result—to be followed by representative institutions. They have, in addition, an English-built and increasing navy, a well-disciplined army, and an efficient police. Legally, their code ought to be one of the foremost in the world; since it will have been the work of several eminent foreign jurists, and been compiled with reference to Western law.[1] And they are not behindhand in more general improvements. Several hundred miles of railway are completed, while many more are to be begun immediately. The introduction of agricultural and other machinery cannot be long delayed; and the labour thus economised may indirectly strengthen their finance (still somewhat entangled by the overflow of paper currency), and gradually inspire that confidence in it for which there is yet some need. As to religion and, to our ideas, the strange immorality of the people, it is more difficult to speak. Until Japan is opened out beyond the six treaty ports,[2] Christian missionaries are confined to a rather precarious field, and the diversity of opinion which they represent forms in itself a serious obstacle to the propagation of their doctrines. If the Japanese adopt Christianity, it is to be feared that they will only do so because they deem it politic to be dressed in the same religious cloak as the nations whom they wish to imitate, and that they will not be actuated by any honest persuasion.

In this mania for Europeanisms, however, there

[1] See p. 59 *ante*.
[2] See p. 59 *ante*, note 2.

are at least two dangers. Firstly, the Government seems to be aiming too high. It cannot expect all at once to thrust upon the people a different mode of life; to introduce an alien language; to supplant the native customs; and to reform the national clothes. The young men are even said to be over-educated, and to be likely to prove insubordinate, from a conviction that they are wiser than their rulers; while the praiseworthy attempts of shop-keepers at English scholarship often result in the quaintest advertisements.[1] All such questions must be a matter of time: and time alone can ensure their success.

And, secondly, there is a danger that the nation will lose its individuality, that it will despise or forget its own peculiar arts and industries in its anxiety to learn the inventions of Europe. Such a catastrophe could only be deeply regretted both by the imitators and the imitated, and it is impossible to believe that the national feeling of the Japanese is not sufficient to avert so irretrievable a disaster.

The progress of Japan during the last twenty years is truly astonishing. The mysteries of its revolution and the extinction of the power of the

---

[1] *e.g.*, UMBRRELL AMAKER. RAILWAY EREIGHT (freight TRNSPORT AGENT. THE TABLES AND THE CHAIRS & WILL SELL CHEAPEST PRICE. HAIRD RESSER.

daimiôs, co-ordinately with the restoration of the Mikado's authority, have no parallel in the history of the world; the acknowledgment of its backwardness, and its subsequent enterprise in treating with European powers, deserve the utmost consideration and respect; and its activity in the introduction of reforms should ultimately succeed in attaining proportionate results.

CHAPTER V.

HONG KONG; CANTON; SINGAPORE; JAVA.

HONG KONG is approached on the north-east through Lyemun Pass. A line of foam often fringes its bare, mountainous gates and rocky shore, and the sea itself ever swarms with the half-conical, awkward sails of countless Chinese junks. Half an hour after passing the entrance, the steamer anchors in the sheltered roadstead, which faces on the north the docks of Kowloon promontory upon the mainland, ceded to us in 1860, and looks southwards upon the clean white houses of Victoria town, with Victoria Peak as a background. Hong Kong is a free port; and it is no small relief to be free from the severities of a custom-house. Most comers there never fail to climb the Victoria Peak, 1,825 feet high, where there is to be found an observatory and signalling station, and a temperature which is all the year round quite eight degrees (Fahr.) cooler than that of the busy town and harbour so close beneath,

Quite recently a tramway has been made up the peak, but visitors can also walk, or be carried by four Chinamen in chairs slung on poles; the path all the way being excellently cemented, and in many places a perfect rockery of tropical plants and trees.[1] From the top, the whole island is fairly visible; it measures about six miles by five, and is little more than a group of barren peaks. Its climate from December to February is very pleasant; in December the weather resembles that of a warm English September; in January it can even be cold enough to make fires acceptable; but from March to November the heat is very exhausting. Its aqueduct—a costly archway and tunnel—which is to supply the town with water from the other side of the island, is an engineering masterpiece; and its Chinatown is characteristic. The forts are not all completely finished, but they are being very well constructed: and some of the guns, as we at home have not been allowed to forget, are very conspicuous by their absence.

Two great problems just now perplex the Government at Hong Kong. They regard its immediate intercourse with China. In the first place, the danger of over-population is imminent, for the area of the island is very small, and there

---

[1] There are a few jin-rikishas in the town, drawn by Chinamen; but they cannot mount the Peak.

is an overflow of Chinese, who very wisely prefer it to their own country. And, secondly, the question of extradition presents unusual difficulties. Offences with them are not offences with us,[1] and our reluctance to hand over certain offenders against Chinese law often drives the Celestial Government to considerable expense, attended very excusably by some irritation. The present *modus vivendi* depends upon the Tientsin treaty of 1858, of which some of the rather vague stipulations may possibly be in need of revision.

However short and however enjoyable one's time may be at Hong Kong—and its residents are sure to make it so—it needs little persuasion to be induced to take the night-boat up the Canton river, and to spend a day or two in Canton. It is reputed one of the most typical towns in China. The small steamer arrives about 6 A.M., to be welcomed by the discordant shouts and sing-song yells incessantly ringing out from the squalid 'sampans' on the river, whose muddy

---

[1] For instance, all the chief official posts, with their valuable pickings, are held by mandarins; and a Chinaman can only become a mandarin by qualifying himself by examination. If a candidate is caught cribbing, it is a capital offence; and, a short time ago, when a son of the Viceroy of Canton was the culprit, even his father's paramount influence could scarcely shield him from the extreme penalty of the law. It is easy to appreciate the hesitation of our authorities before handing over a dishonest examinee. They are sealing his death-warrant for prompt decapitation.

waters are the scenes of constant piracy. The landing-stage is on the embankment of the English 'concession,' a small acreage taken some years ago by us from China for purposes of commerce; and after breakfasting there with a most genial friend, one cannot be better equipped to face the abominations of Canton.

With the help of a guide, it is best to set out in chairs supported by coolies—for reasons which soon become obvious. The wonderfully narrow streets, seldom more and usually less than ten feet wide, are lined with open shops, which are filled with industrious tradesmen, and often reeking with noisome Chinese food. Of this the excellence seems much to depend upon its rawness and state of decay; raw puppy-dogs are a great delicacy; and whiffs of the favourite, well-decayed vegetable are considered extremely delicious. Over these shops, the one-storied houses are generally built of brick, with outhanging perpendicular sign-boards, whose gorgeous tints of red, brown, or yellow, illuminated with golden characters, obscure the light, and seem intended to spread a cloak of duskiness over the dirt below. The granite paving—so slimy as to give a false step very serious consequences—is crowded with hard and sullen faces, one and all a most unpleasing contrast to the smiling Japanese; and it may be doubted how far their expressions about ' fang kwai ' (foreign devils)[1] can be leniently interpreted as complimentary to the passing stranger. The beggars and the smells are alike revolting; and the whole nation is, besides, a race of inveterate gamblers.

Starting round the town to explore some of the more important places, the temple of the five hundred genii conveniently opens the list. It is a comparatively plain, low building, destitute of decoration, except in so far as the long rows of gilded images are in themselves an ornament; and among these, curiously enough, no less a hero than Marco Polo has found his way to a position of divine honour. The execution-ground is probably the next destination. It plays its dismal part at least once in two months, generally much oftener; but its aspect is not ambitious, for it is merely a retired alley, about a hundred yards long by twenty wide, and strewn with pottery baking in the sun. The only water-clock of Canton, quite one of the sights of the town, dwells up a flight of steps, and has been in existence there fully six hundred years. Four pails of water are arranged one above the other, and in the lowest of them a brass rod, marked with Chinese time, is attached to a float, which gradually rises as the water from above flows into the pail. In the Temple of Horrors the ' tableaux,'

---

[1] The ordinary Chinese term for a foreigner. See p. 45 *ante*.

fortunately not *vivants*, but of wood, strikingly portray the ingenious cruelty of Chinese imagination. They represent various tortures in the Buddhist hell, where the wicked are being squeezed between boards, boiled alive, or stewed under a hot bell. Passing on to the old city wall, built of brick and stone twelve hundred years ago, and fortified with obsolete guns, there is a good general view of the city, as well as of the horse-shoe-shaped tombs in the cemetery on an opposing hill. Just beyond, the fifth storey of a large pagoda is a spot well suited for lunch, especially as the picnic takes place under the immediate patronage of two great figures of Confucius and the God of War, to whom a joss-house has there been lately erected. After lunch it is no long distance to the Tartar General's residence, and a nine-storied flower-pagoda. But if serious business is going on in the prefect's court, the horrors of the day are yet to come

This court is the court of appeal next above that of an ordinary magistrate. Down a large four-sided room, with one side open to the air and the public, there are arranged four little tables in single file, each provided with a seat, from which a mandarin is trying a separate case. The prisoners are chained outside in the court-yard behind the public, and brought in when required to crouch before the villainy of the law. The occupation of the court is not uncommonly the trial of pirates, whose momentary offence usually is that they have previously confessed their crime in the lower court, and have since retracted their confession. To extort a fresh avowal no torture is too hideous, no cruelty too severe. In the presence of their judge and everyone in the court the wretches are bambooed on their naked backs in two or three relays of about forty strokes a time, and on continued refusal to admit their guilt are hung from a board by their thumbs and toes, with their knees scarcely touching the ground. Of course, says the guide, their heads will shortly come off; but so strong is their tenacity of life that they will undergo this treatment for several days rather than submit to immediate execution. How brutal a mockery is Chinese justice! Evidence appears to be little sifted except in the magistrate's or lowest court. This official may almost convict a prisoner solely from a grudge that he bears him, for in China he also acts as jury; and when the wretch has been convicted before him, or has confessed his fault (perhaps through the application of torture), a higher tribunal, such as the prefect's court, will seldom set him free,—since it is little better than a court of torture to re-extract confessions of guilt. Bribery is then his best chance. All this arises from an abuse of Confucius's well-meant doctrine that no man may be punished until he has admitted his crime; and in short, while a man in England is innocent until proved to be guilty, in China it is just the reverse.

Of a Chinese jail it is quite sufficient to see two cells, foul with tainted, stifling air. Hordes of squalid prisoners crawl out from these dens of filth, or stretch their thin arms through the rough wooden bars, yelping for the money for which they are allowed to beg, simply so as to provide themselves with better food! And if pity urges the spectator to throw them a few 'cash,' in the hope of alleviating their misery, the present at once becomes the object of a jealous fight. Some of the prisoners are encumbered with 'cangues,' or broad wooden collars; other ill-fed beings have grown almost too weak to move.

From these cages of misery one is thankful to turn to less painful scenes. The Chinese Club or Guild is one of the handsomest buildings in Canton. Its tiles, moulded into elaborate pictures on the roof, its wood-carving, joss-house, and theatre, are all fantastic, and its pillars of carved granite, a really immense work, are quite its most laborious decorations.

The Chinese shops and their industries, especially silk-weaving and flour-grinding, are among the curiosities of Canton; but two or three days there make an ample stay; for 'John's' manners are so reticent, that a year's residence in the town woud hardly fathom the nation's backwardness, diligence, and dirt, or do more to confirm one's worst suspicions about the relentless subtilty of Chinese punishment.

All Chinese read the same characters (excepting the Manchu); but their dialects are so different that a Pekin man and a Cantonese would often prefer to address each other in pidgin English than in their own languages. Fancy, for instance, bargaining about a fly-goose or a sit-down goose instead of a wild or tame one! In their purely commercial dealings with foreigners, Chinese merchants are honest and business-like, and in this respect they compare very favourably with the Japanese.

Leaving Canton, the Portuguese settlement of Macao is about eighty miles down the river, and although it was colonised by Portugal at the beginning of the sixteenth century, it was not recognised by China until 1887. It is a picturesque place, situated on a promontory connected with the mainland by a narrow strip of waste, where an archway or 'barrier' has been erected to mark the termination of Portuguese soil. In its zenith Macao had a flourishing slave trade; but its importance has been ruined by Hong Kong, and it is now the waning residence of unoccupied and uninterested Portuguese. Its dreamy streets are clean and tidy, but it drags on an idle existence, devoid of all plausible object, and supported by a population which is mainly Chinese. Its revenue is derived from the sale of two monopolies, fishing and gambling at a game called 'fantan,' from which the Portuguese Government is said to realise about 30,000*l.* a year, but the tameness of this amusement is well-suited to the dulness of the place. Otherwise, its pride is in the garden of the poet Camoens, who lived to be a contemporary of Shakespeare.

It is a morning's journey to return by sea from Macao to Hong Kong, whence mail steamers —English, French, and German—are continually running southwards for Singapore, there to land passengers, after a six days' voyage, almost in the very midst of the tropics. The landing-stage is two and a half miles from the town; but the native drivers of the 'gharries,' or tiny four-wheeled cabs, each drawn by an active, strong little horse, are always in attendance, and irrepressibly clamorous for employment. In the distance the graceful cocoanut-palms are very plentiful, and along the road the small humpbacked oxen are even more tiny than those in Japan.

Singapore is an island, thirty miles long and

about half as broad, and is the capital of the Straits Settlements.[1] It is eighty miles north of the equator, and was bought by England in 1819 from the Sultan of Johore. It is a free port, and has a population of 100,000, more or less; two thirds of the people are Chinese, and the remainder Klings or Coromandel Coast Indians, Malays, and a few Europeans.[2] This is the first introduction to Malays. Their brilliant turbans look very dazzling in the streets, and their light dresses of red, white, or yellow are equally picturesque. Many wear gold or silver bangles round their arms, but their owners often find that these are troublesome incentives to theft by fellow-natives. Their innate indolence is notorious, and seems inseparable from tropical climates. Their language, it appears, is truly exemplary; it has no grammar, genders, or other school-boy terrors, and is probably the easiest tongue that has ever been spoken;[3] but poverty of language nearly always indicates poverty of ideas, and certainly the Malay race is no exception to the rule.

The curse of Singapore is its snakes and its

---

[1] The Straits Settlements also include Penang, Wellesley Provinces, and Malacca.
[2] The Klings are the Tamils of India.
[3] For instance, everything is singular unless its repetition makes it plural. Thus 'orang' means 'man'; if you wish to speak of 'men,' you must say 'orang-orang.'

tigers. Many of the latter will swim a mile from the mainland to roam about its dense jungles; whilst other vermin are no less prolific, and the ubiquitous mosquito, the incarnation of persistency, never fails to dispute the possession of one's bedroom and one's bed. The vegetation is quite beautiful, luxuriant in a perpetual hothouse and perpetual spring; for there are no seasons, and the leaves are at once ever green and ever falling. All the year round the sun rises and sets about six o'clock, and the absence of twilight, so invariably an attribute of the tropics, is sometimes very inconvenient to the evening arrangements of a northern stranger. In half an hour an inky night is transformed into a glaring day, and before long 80° Fahr. is the average temperature in the shade. When it rains it usually does so but a short time, but its downpour is furious while it lasts.

The wild flowers in every hedge are so handsome that it is difficult to persuade oneself that they are not all cultivated, and the varied colours of the butterflies, as they flit from place to place, brighten every corner of the thick and clayey jungles. The damp and sultry heat, however, is at midday rather enervating; but to it, as to mosquitoes, the traveller slowly gets acclimatised. Among the beauties of the Botanical Gardens are the cocoanut-palm, banana trees, the tall *spathodea* with its fiery scarlet flowers, and the gigantic fan-shaped travellers' palm, which is peculiarly indigenous to the island. The queen of the bushes in every garden is the *hibiscus*, whose five-petalled flowers of brilliant crimson radiate from a small orange plume; while the plants include the eucharis lily, delicate maidenhairs, and numberless precious rarities. The Experimental Garden produces samples of sugar-canes, indigo, nutmeg, and a hedge of logwood. The three great fruits of Singapore are pine-apples, which grow in the fields in long rows like so many cabbages; the dark red apple-shaped mangusteens; and the large durians, which have a smell so disgusting that it may take one several years to acquire the courage to taste them, though their enlisted supporters will not hear of such abuse.

The Governor of the crown colony of the Straits Settlements is assisted in his government by an executive council of fourteen members, whose discussions are cabinet secrets. All the members, however, belong *ex officio* to the legislative council of twenty-one, which holds its debates in public. The successful finances of the colony are almost proverbial, and are greatly due to the trade of Chinamen, who are a very peaceable ingredient of the population. When, however, a Chinaman is insubordinate, the governor can send for him and examine him before the executive council, and, upon sufficient evidence, he has a most useful power of 'deporting' him as a bad character to his own country, where 'John' is shrewd enough to know that his head is far less safe than in Singapore, and that in any case his commercial profits will flag.

If occasion offers, it is instructive to 'put in an appearance' at the colonial assizes. The jury, it is at once observable, only consists of seven; and very wisely, considering the temperature, nobody dreams of a wig. When a Chinese witness is sworn in, he undergoes a ceremony of holding up one of his hands, but this is a mere solemn formality to remind him of the existence of prosecutions for perjury, since his religion prescribes nothing to bind him. Interpreters are, of course, indispensable.

The forts of the colony are admirably concealed, and are daily expecting guns from home: and it seems that some of these might with advantage have been ordered to command a longer range, if only the army estimates had allowed it.

With a fortnight or so to spare about Singapore, the time cannot slip away more pleasantly than by a trip to Java, whither Dutch or French boats are bound every week, on a sea-passage which lasts two days.

From the port of Tandjong Priok, the railway runs eight miles to Batavia, the capital of Java and of the Dutch East Indies. It passes in many places through a dense and swampy jungle, where cassia-trees and towering cocoanut-palms, laden with fruit, are thriving in tropical glory, and with which it is not hard to associate the growls of some roaming tiger. But in the scattered town of Batavia there is not much to see. Everywhere the muddy canals are a sure sign of Dutch possession, and the very respectable houses of Chinese merchants in one quarter are such as could never exist in China, for there they would only betray to the mandarins that their owners were fit persons to be 'fleeced.' The Malay dresses are much more gay than the sombre blue of Japan; but the many idle loungers, who sit cross-legged on their doorsteps and smoke their pipes, are a severe contrast to the bustling subjects of the Mikado. The Malay houses are usually thatched cottages, with an open front and only a ground floor, and they are frequently raised on posts about a foot from the earth, to prevent, as far as possible, the uninvited calls of snakes and other vermin. Malay food is little else than rice and fruit, and includes none of the nasty raw meat or fish so common in China. Their cattle are a variety of the Indian buffalo.

In the Batavian museum are to be seen many strange oriental swords, gods, flags, and coins, from Java, Borneo, Siam, and other places, besides large musical instruments made of bamboo, which might well be mistaken for unwieldy toys.

Thirty miles inland from Batavia is the town of Buitenzorg, the Simla, though an inferior one, of the Dutch Governor-General. Just in front of his house are the public botanical gardens, with a fine avenue of banyan-trees (*ficus*), and a pond full of lotus-flowers and large Victoria regia lilies. The palms, too, are magnificent, and the fine collection of orchids would excite the envy of many collectors.

From Buitenzorg to Bandong the line curves along round several dormant or extinct volcanoes, every now and then passing coffee, tea, or sugar plantations, or skimming over rice-fields, which are always arranged in artificial terraces to secure their more perfect irrigation. As usual, the palms, bamboos, and banana-trees are profuse: and on the latter is sometimes growing their dull red flower, weighed down by clusters of green fruit— which, by the way, is not allowed to ripen until it has been picked. The papaw-trees also bear a most wholesome fruit, having the taste of a juiceless melon; and the sap of the tree has the singular property of making the toughest meat

View of Mount Salak from Buitenzorg, Java.

quite tender, even after it has only been *hung* near it for a short time.

The elevation of Bandong, at 2,200 feet, produces a temperature by no means unpleasant. Indeed, the climate of Java inland, considering its tropical position, is unexpectedly cool and healthy; for it is high and mountainous; and, although the island is 660 miles long, no part of it is more than seventy miles from the sea.

While staying at Bandong, a ramble up the dormant volcano of Tankoebanprahoe [1] is the lot of every traveller. The day begins with a nine-mile drive to Lembang, probably in a small carriage with three little horses abreast, where government plantations, both of coffee and cinchona, are very successfully grown. The coffee looks like, and is, a dark species of laurel with white, scented flowers and green berries: the under leaves of the cinchona tree, which averages about twenty feet in height, are often a handsome red. Its bark when peeled off to make quinine, can form afresh; but the second and subsequent growths are not so good as the first. The endless coffee plantations in the district, necessarily shaded by larger trees, belong mainly to the Government; the thickest bushes are now eight or ten years old; and in the best soil they will

[1] Oe in Dutch is pronounced u.

live for fifty. The bushes in Java were originally imported from Mocha, and these never grow well in any but virgin soil. Their green berries turn red towards April, and in May the crop is gathered.

To return. The ascent of the volcano (6,500 feet above the sea) from Lembang is a long ride through an exceedingly dense and beautiful jungle, crowded with large trees and big ferns, palms, and tropical creepers. On nearing the top, the fumes of sulphur are unmistakable, as they come up from two adjoining craters, each gaping open like a wide deserted pit. Their upper edge is lined with lava, and lower down, near the film of rain-water at the bottom, slight curls of smoke keep oozing out from the sulphury crust. Towards these the spirit of adventure challenges a scramble, and—possibly at the imminent risk of an eruption!—the theft of a few yellow crystals from several places where the temperature is quite warm enough to boil an egg. The views are exceedingly pretty: looking back, especially, from the slopes on the east of the volcano, the soft hues of the distant heights blend almost imperceptibly with their wooded foreground on the plains of Bandong. The town may be reached again by a different road, after stopping at Lembang for tea—or other refreshment, as Java tea is rather acrid.

Taking the train back towards Batavia, as far as Tjiandjoer, there is a lovely day's drive across country between that place and Buitenzorg, along which, as might be expected, the views again are perfectly enchanting; and the chains of rugged peaks, which stand out behind the rich and luxuriant plains, line a succession of panoramas, quite as indescribable as they are extensive. The sides of the road are much planted with tiny trees, some day perhaps destined to become a famous avenue; and the hedges are glowing with bright clusters of the orange *lantana*, a plant to be seen at home only in our hottest hothouses, but in Java an incorrigible weed. Dotted about the landscape, also, the occasional native cottages of bamboo and thatch look as casual as their listless occupiers. Fourteen miles from Tjiandjoer is a healthily situated military hospital, managed *under contract* for the Government; and that the contractor takes an interest in his work is proved by his having provided the hospital with a billiard-table, an amateur theatre, and every possible comfort; besides which, he turns an honest penny as the proprietor of the hotel close by. After lunching there, and possibly smoking a Javanese cigarette, which consists of rather coarse tobacco rolled up in light palm-bark, the excursionist is fresh to continue his drive. Further on, it is worth while to leave the road and walk to a narrow lake, and although, in the rainy season, it is rather disturbing to find that the grassy path which leads to it serves also the purpose of a watercourse, the rewards of the effort are a pretty strip of water at the foot of a wooded precipice, and an impenetrable thickness of glossy jungle through which the way is cut. Buitenzorg is in sight towards sunset, and trains are continually returning to Batavia and its harbour.

With six weeks to spare in Java, it would be inexcusable to miss the world-famed Buddhist ruins at Bora-boedoor, in the centre of the island, or the magnificent scenery and volcanoes at its eastern end. But in the present unfinished condition of the government railways, it is not easy to see the island completely in a shorter time; and, with no longer time available, the best course is to sail back to Singapore.

The twenty million population of Java is chiefly Malay, with a sprinkling of Chinese, and a few Europeans and half-castes; the natives of the island include four distinct races, each of which speaks a different language. Strangely enough, Dutch is nowhere encouraged, partly with a view of preventing the blacks from prying into their masters' business, and partly because it is considered impudent for them to address a Dutchman in it. As to religion, the native people now mostly profess Mahomedanism; but up to 1478 Hindooism and Buddhism were prevalent, and some of the old Buddhist remains—especially those already referred to at Bora-boedoor—are very interesting memorials.

European living in Java is expensive, but for a native, rice supplies most of his wants and is extremely cheap, an ordinary well-paid labourer subsisting comfortably on five pence a day. Even the meal of a native prince or regent is not extravagant. The *pièce de résistance* is intensely heavy cakes of the customary half-steamed rice, to be flavoured with dry curry, jerked beef,[1] shrimps, treacle, or cold half-boiled eggs, as fancy may prompt, but for much of which courtesy or curiosity can alone lend strangers an appetite. If justice be done to the meal, the only antidote is unlimited exercise.

The government of the island is nominally, very nominally, a despotism, under a native Emperor who lives at Soerakarta, and a Sultan at Djokjakarta, besides native regents in each province, who are all nonentities enjoying hereditary sinecures. But the Dutch have been really in undisturbed possession since the beginning of the seventeenth century, with the exception of a short

[1] Jerked-beef is beef preserved by drying in the sun.

period between 1811 and 1816, when England occupied the country during the absorption of Holland by the Napoleonic wars. Our governor, who was subordinate to Lord Minto as Governor-General of India, was Sir Stamford Raffles, afterwards the founder of Singapore.

The present Dutch government is directed by the Governor-General sent out from Holland, in theory during the king's pleasure, but in practice for five years, to enjoy a salary of over 13,000*l*. a year. A council of five members assists him, and under its supervision each of the twenty-two provinces is ruled by a Dutch resident, who professes to be merely advising the native regent of the province.

The peculiar culture system, or system of forced labour, imposed by the Dutch Government in Java, was established in 1832, but its administration is too intricate to be examined very precisely here. In general, however, the natives have to work for the Government a definite period of time every year, and, for the purpose of being employed at different kinds of labour, or of working different periods of time in the year, they are divided into classes, of which that doing the maximum average of compulsory work labours one day in seven, and that doing the minimum average ten days in the year. The wages are very low, and in the production of coffee, which is disposed of by auction (presumably in Amsterdam), the Government realise the enormous profit of 300 per cent. There are, however, also private plantations of coffee, which compete to some extent with those of the Government; but on them there is no forced labour, and the profits of the owners are, in consequence, not nearly so large. This 'culture system' is enforced upon the people either by a twenty-five shillings fine for each refusal (no small sum to a native), or else a week's imprisonment; and it constitutes an essential difference between the English and the Dutch methods of governing a colony. The pervading idea of the Dutch is trade, and their policy is to turn native labour to the best advantage for Holland; our motive, it is to be hoped, is rather to raise the life and condition of the people, and to encourage the activity of native merchants.

How long, then, it may be asked, can such a system last without convulsion? Both on Europeans and Javanese the taxes are exceedingly heavy, and the low pay of smaller officials has tempted them to practise extortion. For sixteen years, also, unknown to most of us, the Dutch have been waging a desultory war in Acheen against the natives of Sumatra; but as no serious effort has been made to end it—indeed, certain contractors are probably interested in keeping it up—its long continuance is beginning to shake the belief of easterns that their Dutch rulers are invincible. But though some discontent may be rife, it needs much oppression to arouse the natural indolence of the Malay ; and it is more likely that Java will only change hands through the embroilment of Holland in a European war than from any internal cause. To whomsoever the island belongs the fertility of its soil will always make it a very valuable possession.

CHAPTER VI.

CEYLON AND SOUTHERN INDIA.

ON returning to Singapore, the mails and passengers are despatched weekly to Ceylon; either by a P. and O., which allows a few hours at Penang, a German steamer, or a French 'Messageries,' which goes direct to Colombo. Besides a steam-whistle, one or two of the latter are provided with a siren, an instrument whose sneeze is never to be forgotten when once heard, especially if, on arriving about 4 A.M., one is either among the sleeping inhabitants of Colombo, or the dozing inmates of the ship itself. The passage takes about five days.

The railway from Colombo to Kandy is one of the most beautiful in Ceylon and in the world; but from the station of Rambukkana, where the gradient becomes a steeper one, the scenery is perfectly enchanting. As it winds along, it leaves below or behind it wooded and rocky glens, deepening into irregular valleys, from which the cocoa-nut lifts its stately head amid an ocean of tropical beauty. Sometimes the picture is wide

and extensive, often more narrow and indented.
Here and there is a tea or cinchona plantation, or
natives are plodding away up to their knees in
water, wading in the terraced rice-fields; while
on every bank the orange lantana-weed spreads a
carpet of glittering stars. Kandy is reached in
time. Its situation is delightfully secluded, close
to a small artificial lake, and shut in by cosy hills.
Its houses are generally tiled, with a single ground
floor, from the entrance to which the squatting
natives idly watch every intruding carriage. And
how amazing it is to be free from Chinamen, who
have pursued the traveller since San Francisco!
The population is Singhalese, with a large infusion
of Tamil Indians, who are a fine-looking race, and
by far the more industrious of the two. The men
usually wear long hair, often bound back by a
semicircular comb; and some of them wear red or
white turbans.

The nucleus of Buddhism in Ceylon is the
temple of Buddha's tooth at Kandy. It is dedicated
to a relic which is scarcely ever shown, but the
authenticity of which it would be sacrilegious to
dispute, although its size is rumoured to bear
comparison with that of an elephant's tusk! The
building is utterly different to the temples of
Japan, and its stone walls are painted with curious
ancient designs. Inside, a crystal image of a

seated Buddha inhabits a beautifully-carved silver and ivory casket; but the great mainstay of the temple is the shrine of the tooth, which is preserved in an artistic golden bell, itself caged and padlocked. Close by are kept some valuable presents of gold and silver from a pious king of Kandy; and in an adjoining building is the audience-hall of these former kings, with ninety-seven elaborate wooden pillars, now sadly degenerated to perform the functions of a district court of justice.

About three miles from the town are the Kandy Botanical Gardens. They are very neatly laid out, bordering on a river, and much more picturesque than those at Buitenzorg, while their palms are quite as fine. Among their many specimens are the pale yellow plum-shaped nutmeg, ebony and india-rubber trees, the radiant scarlet flowers of the *amherstia* tree, and bunches of cloves, resembling budding sprays of jessamine. The spice—it is not always realised—is the buds, and not the seeds, of the clove-bush. There are also sago-palms, from whose pith sago is extracted; magnificent bushes of bamboo, the favourite haunts of poisonous snakes; and dark red beans of the cacao, which in their raw state have not the faintest taste of chocolate. There is no connection, it may be mentioned, between cocoa-nuts, cocoa, and coca. Cocoa-nuts grow on the tall cocoa-nut palm; they can be eaten as fruit, but in the East are generally preferred in curries; and the natives are very fond of their juice or milk, which has a flavour disappointingly like sweetened water. Cocoa, or cacao, is prepared from a bean which grows on a cacao-bush. Coca is a medical drug obtained from the leaves of a shrub originally found in South America.

Returning to Colombo, the canals of the town cannot fail to suggest that it was once a Dutch colony. In the streets, the native conveyances are primitive; the bullocks which draw them do their work most gallantly, and are driven by perfect Jehus. From Colombo a small steamer plies once a week to Tuticorin in Southern India.

With the merest glimpse both of Ceylon and Java, an opinion as to their respective merits can only be given for what it is worth; but the exquisite detail in the scenery of Ceylon seems, as it were, to contain a deeper insight into nature than the very sublime and extensive panoramas of Java. On the other hand, the luxuriance of Java jungles has no equal in Ceylon.

Ceylon is one of the chief of our crown colonies, and has a population of nearly three millions. The average temperature at Colombo is 81° Fahr.; the average rainfall there is 87 inches;

and the driest months in the island are January, February, and March. In London the average rainfall is about 21 inches.

As to its history, the Singhalese are said to have been in the ascendency from B.C. 543, when they emigrated from the valley of the Ganges, to A.D. 1815, when the English dethroned the last king of Kandy. The Portuguese first visited the island in 1505, but did not form a permanent settlement there till 1517. They were driven out by the Dutch in 1658. England captured it in 1796, during the great European war which followed the French Revolution, and placed it under the control of the East India Company. In 1798, however, it was declared a colony of the British Crown, although it was not formally annexed to it until the peace of Amiens in 1802. A petty warfare continued notwithstanding with the king of Kandy, who had never been subdued either by Portuguese or Dutch, their possessions having extended only along the sea-coast and low country, till at length, after numerous outrages, the English adopted stringent measures against him, and in March 1815 George III. was proclaimed king of the whole island. Two small rebellions have since broken out, in 1817 and 1848.

The government, quite independent of that of India, is administered by a governor and an executive council of five members. For laws, supplies, &c., there is a legislative council of fifteen, ten being officials (including the members of the executive council), and six unofficials, appointed to represent the various interests of race and trade. As the governor can always command the votes of the officials, the government always holds a majority in reserve, but the publicity given to the meetings of the council is sufficient to prevent any arbitrary decision. The eight provinces of the island are divided and subdivided under government agents.

The religion of Ceylon is Buddhist, but it is adulterated with Hindoo idol-worship, and is less pure than the Buddhism of Burmah and Siam, and it is not identical with that of Japan and China. The Singhalese, too, are painfully superstitious, and pay great respect to demon-worship.

Much of the island is cultivated, especially with paddy (rice) fields. Tea, to suit the whims of the London market, is steadily displacing the earlier coffee, and cocoa-nuts, cinchona, cocoa, and cinnamon all add their quota to the general abundance; yet the soil, as a whole, is much poorer than that in Java. There is no land tax such as the land tax in India, but rice-fields in private ownership pay a tax of one-tenth of their produce. In a few cases, however, as a reward for loyal services, it has been reduced to one-fourteenth, or even remitted in perpetuity. Tea, coffee, and cocoa do not pay any tax.

The wild elephants are more or less protected by law. Many pearl oysters are found in the Gulf of Mannár, and many precious stones are for sale in Colombo; also—particularly for the benefit of verdant tourists—their fraudulent imitations in Birmingham glass.

When within sight of a speck of sand, a few trees, and a distant lighthouse, the steamer is announced to have reached Tuticorin, and in a small steam-launch passengers have to risk a six-mile toss over the coral reefs which endanger that coast of India. Tuticorin is only a village, and it is best to take the first train for Mādūra, though the South Indian Railway is without exception the worst in the country. Its carriages are excruciating; its joltings very severe: and it is altogether very fortunate that it is shortly to be taken over by the government. Travelling first-class, may be seen a native zemindár or landlord, dressed, perhaps, in a loose, white gown with showy facings of gold; and among the crowds of dark Tamils at the stations many handsome faces loiter about, watching for any friends in the train. The crops include much cotton and some coriander seed, the latter always useful in curries; and by the side of the railway the prickly spikes of a bluish-grey hedge of magnificent aloes present a formidable barrier both to men and cattle. The country is very flat.

On arriving at Madura there turns out to be no hotel, and the best available bedrooms are over the station; but if an hotel did exist, and it was no better than most others in India, its absence would be scarcely felt! The houses are of brick or white-washed mud, and the natives in the streets and throughout India beautify themselves with nose-rings, ear-rings, bracelets, and bangles, generally of gold or silver, and some of the ladies even go so far as to smear their faces with turmeric. The waggons, as in Colombo, are drawn by bullocks, animals held in the greatest veneration, and never eaten by the Hindoos, and in January their horns are painted red, green, or black, in honour of the feast of bullocks, which is annually solemnised according to the rights of the Hindoo religion. A guide will point out many Brahmins, the highest caste or rank of Hindoos. These intermarry only among themselves, and never eat food with any of the other three castes, still less with Europeans. They mix, nevertheless, with the other castes, and a Brahmin cook occupies somewhat the same position as a French *chef* at home.

Madura is famous for its great Hindoo temple, dedicated to Síva, one of the persons of the Hindoo Trinity, and to the goddess Minyáchi. It was

restored three hundred years ago by an illustrious
rajah, and is now kept in magnificent repair by the
native merchants and bankers of the town. Its
eight or nine pagodas[1] are all covered with small
painted figures of chunam or Madras stucco, and
every figure represents the subject of some mytho-
logical tale. Inside the temple there are innumerable corridors of stone pillars, elaborately carved
into big gods, horses, or monsters; and daily
during each January a procession creeps forth in
honour of the god and goddess Siva and Minyáchi,
who are seated in palanquins, and preceded by
sacred elephants and an appalling din, in celebra-
tion of their annual festival. Beggars, as everywhere, are a perfect pest, whining at all the
doorways; and it does not improve one's temper
to know that many of them are well off, and only
too artful not to turn to good account the presence
of a European.

The three persons of the Hindoo Trinity are
Brahma, the creator, Vishnu, the preserver, and
Siva, the destroyer: and in the Madura temple Siva
is annually married to Minyáchi, the aboriginal
goddess of Southern India, the pair forming the
bulwark of this branch of Hindooism. It is rather
a kind of social philosophy than any definite

[1] Indian and Japanese pagodas are almost invariably sacred
edifices; those in China are often simple monuments.

creed; and as the many native tribes have engrafted upon it their own peculiar myths, the whole theology has now become a very unfathomable jumble.

Many costly jewels are the property of the temple, and the great wooden images of elephants and bullocks are thickly plated with gold or silver. In one of the court-yards there is a sacred tank or pond of dirty green water, almost daily washed in and even drunk by pious devotees, so that the height of the cholera death-rate is no great matter for surprise.

Passing on, a native guide to the town will proudly expatiate upon the old palace, now used as government offices, the square sacred tank, one of the largest in India, and an enormous banyan-tree, only seventy feet high, but spreading out its branches two hundred yards in circumference; and these it supports by its own upright suckers, stretching downwards like poles fixed in the ground.

Trichinopoly, a place renowned in history, is not far north of Madura. It saw the early career of Clive, and in 1752 was the scene of his successes under Major Lawrence in their joint operations against the French. With the rest of the Carnatic it became a British possession in 1801 : and it is now the resting-place of Bishop Heber, who was drowned there in his bath-room in 1826, having been appointed Bishop of Calcutta but two years before. He is supposed to have been seized with a fit.

The rock of Trichinopoly, nearly 600 feet high, is a faint reproduction of Edinburgh Castle, and is crowned with a small temple belonging to Siva. It is a fine solitary mass, formerly a garrisoned fort, which rises from the very heart of the town, and commands a glorious view of the fertile cocoa-nuts, tobacco-crops, and paddy-fields in the surrounding plain. On one side is the distant outline of the Eastern Ghauts, with the windings of the river Káveri in the foreground; and just beyond its sandy stream the pagodas of the Srí-rangam temple tower over the groves of palm-trees. The town is reputed to be one of the hottest places in India, and even in winter the thermometer registers 90° in the shade. It is famous for its silver-work, tobacco, and cheroots.

Five miles away, between the rivers Káveri and Coleroon, is the large Hindoo temple at Srí-rangam, dedicated to Vishnu. The outermost of its seven square walls has a circumference of four miles! and it contains some twenty pagodas, across which, at rapid intervals, green parrots dart swiftly from palm to palm. Throughout India many Hindoos have a custom of smearing their foreheads every morning with bright-coloured powders, to designate their religious caste or sect, or to show that they have said their prayers; and in the streets near this temple the number of foreheads painted with the peculiar mark of Vishnu show his followers to be very numerous in the locality.

From Trichinopoly to Tanjore is but a short distance eastwards. It literally possesses no accommodation for travellers (not so rare a complaint in the 'benighted presidency'), so that it is highly

VISHNU MARK, SMEARED BY THE HINDOOS ON THEIR FOREHEADS.

expedient to curtail one's visit there as far as possible; for unless some hospitable resident takes pity upon one's homeless condition, the night may conceivably be spent in chairs on the station platform, in the company of mosquitoes and dirt.

The great feature at Tanjore is another and remarkable temple, reached by a drive in a seatless and rickety country cart, which is the best public carriage of a town with 50,000 inhabitants. It is entered through two archways scattered with Hindoo images; and, though not very large, the

The Great Pagoda, Tanjore, Southern India

privacy of its situation and the very tasteful proportions of its fine pagoda give it the victory over its rivals at Madura and Trichinopoly. It is said to be three or four thousand years old, and is considered one of the finest specimens of Hindoo architecture throughout India. In front of the pagoda is a monstrous bull, 12 feet 10 inches high, and 20 feet 9 inches long, cut from a single block of black granite, which, by some unknown contrivance, the early builders managed to transport to its present situation. The large pagoda itself stands on a base of ornamented granite, from which its elegant decorations taper like a pyramid to a height of 200 feet, and culminate in a round summit hewn out of one piece of granite and capped with a gilded pinnacle. The effect is exceedingly handsome. The granite weighs no less than twelve tons; and its elevated position, like the bull on its pedestal, pays a high tribute to the skill of ancient engineers. Not the least curious decoration on the pagoda is the head of a European with a billicock hat, which must have been inserted there by some native admirer! The neat court-yard of the temple contains also some smaller pagodas with finely-wrought granite carving, besides a gallery of equestrian and other paintings of the Mahratta rajahs of Tanjore, whose dynasty became extinct in 1855. The wall of the court-yard is adorned with pictures of Hindoo legends, equally grotesque in idea and execution; but no Indian temple has any similarity to those in Japan.

One of the sights of the place is a dirty tank, close to a church built in 1777 by the assiduity of Swartz, the German pioneer of Christian missionaries to the East; and he is memorialised inside in a monument by Flaxman.

The old palace of the former rajahs of Tanjore has a fine durbar or assembly-hall, with architecture which savours of being at once half-Moorish and half-Hindoo, and there is also a gorgeous court-house. The library contains several curious books, one of them cleverly illustrative of Darwinism.

The fertility of the Tanjore district has earned for it the distinction of being called the granary of Southern India, and it supplies one-tenth of the revenue of the Madras presidency. The natives carry on as well an extensive manufacture of silver and copper trays, inlaid with idols of different metals, but the study of the empty upstair regions in which they are sold is no sort of equivalent for the time squandered in bargaining for them. They are handsome, certainly, though rather massive, but criticism should be lenient, for the native artisans are working to supply an English and absent market, and to please a nation whose tastes they are not acquainted with, and whose appliances they do not understand.

Perhaps it is worth while to deviate for a day or two from the main line to Madras, just to look in at Pondicherry. The country near it is very flat and jungleless. Many are the fields of rice; in others the natives are ploughing with teams of either bullocks or Indian buffaloes, and occasionally there is sufficient pasture for a flock of brown Indian sheep, whose mutton is rather coarse. Among the trees are numbers of palmyra palms, and intruding near the railway, besides the aloe hedge with its tall telegraph-post flowers, are several plants of the cactus or prickly pear.

Pondicherry is a first-rate type of an obsolete French colony, and a substantial proof of their misfortunes in directing or consolidating their settlements. They seem unable to comprehend their colonies, and their ill-success mainly springs from ideas of over-government, and from a want of sympathy with the local interests. The place is neat and clean, but nevertheless it looks dilapidated and forlorn, and everywhere the paint is peeling off the houses. It has its custom-house, of course, and a few dark Algerian soldiers guard its public offices; but it has scarcely any trade, and its decay is hardly second to Macao. There is really nothing to see, except two or three French flags, and it is just to realise that nothingness that it is worth a visit. It possesses a rather handsome statue of Dupleix, the opponent of Lord Clive, on a carved and granite pedestal carried off from a neighbouring temple, a lighthouse, a pier, and some indifferent botanical gardens, where water is stealthily springing up from an Artesian well. Like Madras, it has no harbour. The position of the town was bought by the French from a native rajah in 1672, and has been retaken several times by England. Its population, which is almost entirely native, is now about 19,000.

To go on to Madras is to make a comparison between the conqueror and the conquered, to raise the curtain upon the prospects of Pondicherry had fortunes been reversed a century ago. Yet Madras is a sprawling town, covering an enormous area, from which the public buildings peep out amid a maze of cocoa-nut palms; and it is strange, even for the capital of the benighted presidency, that it should positively be destitute of gas. The surf in the roadstead is a by-word, and in the case of a gale, anchored ships have to run out to sea; but Fort St. George commands genuine respect as the first permanent settlement of England in India. Though its ramparts are useless now, it has fought many foes, and negotiated and intrigued with

Nawabs of the Carnatic and Nizams of Hyderabad. Once it was captured by the French under Labourdonnais in 1746, but was restored two years later at the treaty of Aix-la-Chapelle. Since then it has trained and nurtured Clive, it has checked the ambition of Dupleix, it has put a stop to the depredations of Hyder Ali, it has spread the peace of British rule throughout the Coromandel coast, and now the busy city around it is the lasting trophy of its achievements.

The public buildings of the city generally shown are the post-office, the university, and the revenue-office, formerly a Nawab's palace. Government House is a fine building, and, close to it, the State Banqueting Hall has a handsome interior hung with flags and the pictures of former worthies, the governors of Madras.

CHAPTER VII.

NORTHERN INDIA: FROM CALCUTTA TO DELHI.

FEW hurrying 'globe-trotters' would be intent upon going from Madras to Calcutta by rail. The journey involves a circuit up to within a few miles of Bombay, in very hot and dusty trains, while a three days' passage by P. and O. is scarcely longer, and infinitely more cool, pleasant, and sociable.

For vessels of heavy tonnage the navigation of the eighty miles up the Hoogly before reaching Calcutta is in places exceedingly dangerous, and the large amount of shipping passing to and fro also requires every captain to be continually on the alert. Could the metropolis be re-founded, or floated down the river, it would no doubt take up a position nearer the sea, which would be far more convenient to all concerned; but the nucleus of Calcutta was three little villages which were among our earliest settlements,[1] and our colonists dared

---

[1] Chutanutti, Govindpore, and Kálighát. Kálighát, the ghát or landing-place of the goddess Kali, wife of Síva, is the origin of the name Calcutta.

not at that time be too punctilious in accepting favours from the Nawab of Bengal.

Calcutta is renowned as the city of palaces, a dignity which its stately structures, columns, parks, and statues have very justly contributed to bestow. On the left bank of the Hoogly the last King of Oudh's palace is conspicuous, and not far from it there are to be found some valuable samples in the botanical gardens. On the right bank Fort William figures as the largest fortress in India; and on the same side the pretty Eden garden is *the* proper resort for an evening walk— except on one day in the week, when the tyranny of fashion and a military band compel the world to sit in their carriages outside. The 'Zoo' owns two man-eating tigers; and the museum will soon have nothing to covet: but the native portion of the town is disappointing. Of the 'Black Hole' the site is only discernible by a small pavement at the north-east end of the general post-office, but it marks a crime so atrocious that centuries will not efface the thrill that electrified Europe at the first report of its news.

Government House, with a palatial exterior, is all state-rooms and corridors, and has inside a very limited accommodation. It was built by Lord Wellesley; and not the least stately of its rooms is the council-chamber, used every Friday morning when the Viceroy is in residence at Calcutta. Last spring, the discussions of the Council, under the presidency of Lord Dufferin, were animated by proposals for an increased duty upon the importation of salt and petroleum. Eloquent, altogether, they were not; the set speeches are merely read; but, if the opinion may be expressed without presumption, they more than mastered the situation in perspicuity and learning. The Council unanimously agreed that the unwelcome tax should be imposed, in order to counteract the steady diminution which has recently affected the revenues of India. The temporary causes of this deficit are, more especially, the deterioration of the rupee, and the newly-started Chinese competition in opium. In addition to these the annexation of Upper Burmah, though highly profitable and advantageous in the future, has for the moment augmented the expenditure of the empire; and lately, too, a considerable outlay has been incurred in the North-West Provinces. The Council argued, with convincing force, that indirect is far better suited to India than direct taxation, on the ground that it is not easy to arrive at the amount of native fortunes, and that the collection of an income-tax in India is in itself a costly incident.

The council-chamber is a high room, hung

round the doors and windows with tall red and gold curtains. Two long side-tables for the members of the council are joined at the top by a cross-table, at the centre of which sits the Viceroy; and at the further end of the room two rows of chairs are intended for the public. On the Viceroy's right sits the Commander-in-Chief in India, the Lieut.-Governor of Bengal, the finance minister, and three or four others; on his left are about twelve unofficial members (*i.e.* not members of the executive council), and among them four natives, who make able and influential speeches, notwithstanding their disadvantage in using a foreign language. Behind the Viceroy's chair is a famous picture of Warren Hastings: and the proceedings are very properly watched from the wall by Lord Clive, Lord Cornwallis, Lord Wellesley, and Lord Minto, and there are also smaller pictures of Lords Hardinge and Elgin.

The government of India is vested in the Governor-General (Viceroy) in Council, supervised by the Secretary of State for India at home. He has an executive council of six members, and a legislative one of about twenty, including the six members of the executive; and, as he can override his council even when it is unanimous, his work and responsibility must be far from being light. Over all the dominions of the Empire the Governor-

General in Council has more or less power, varying according as they are governorships, lieut.-governorships, chief-commissionerships, &c. In the Madras and Bombay presidencies there are governors, each with executive and legislative councils, and Lord Connemara and Lord Reay hold, in their own sphere, a position of much greater importance than the lieut.-governors do in theirs; for the governors communicate directly with the Government at home. No lieut.-governor has an executive council; but in Bengal and (recently) in the North-West Provinces, the lieut.-governor has been granted a legislative council, being himself up to a certain point the sole executive: in the Punjaub the lieut.-governor acts without any councils. In the Central Provinces the chief-commissioner is unassisted by councils, and at present the arrangement is the same in Burmah. The administration of the native states is directed and approved by a British resident; and in Indore the Maharajah's government is controlled by an Agent-Governor-General. Police, &c., in such cases is in the hands of natives; but the Agent-Governor-General may always interfere at his discretion, and report or complain to the Viceroy in Council. Such a complaint would probably be followed by a caution, and continued obstinacy or incompetence on the part of the native prince would be usually met by a curtailment of his powers.

Fourteen miles up the Hoogly from Calcutta is the Viceroy's delightfully English residence at Barrackpore; but nothing short of hill-stations like Simla or Darjeeling can moderate an Indian June. Although the plains of Calcutta are only just in the tropics, their heat in summer is unbearable; but with Darjeeling it is otherwise, in its Himalayan seclusion, 7,300 feet above the sea. The road by the Darjeeling-Himalayan railway, which climbs to it from Siliguri fifty miles, is a wonderful work, and deserves a passing notice. Were it not insulting, it might almost be called a toy line, as it is only provided with a 2-ft. gauge; but its sturdy little engines and lilliputian carriages fulfil their duty admirably, and might even astonish American genius. It lies like a tramway along the waggon road, several of its curves having actually a radius of 70 feet; and, as it rises about 1,000 feet in every seven miles, its speed is wisely limited to an average of 7 miles an hour.

About six miles beyond Siliguri the Himalayan ascent begins, and with it tea-plantations, a rapid fall of the thermometer, and very frequently fog and rain. To see the views from Darjeeling really well is a great piece of luck; constantly the snows of the Himalayas are buried in cloud for days together, and one's dreams are a tantalising blank. Sometimes the mountains are more considerate and show themselves by transient instalments, fancifully connected by links of drifting mist; but even then the imagination is left to clothe the gaps which it does not see with guesses from what it does. On such occasions it is almost dark on being awakened at six o'clock, when the broad peak of Kinchinjanga, 45 miles away, 28,000 feet high, and in its height second only to Mount Everest, is already peering above the silent ocean of haze below. It is guarded on either side by its more slender satellites, and as their crystal outline grows clearer, its fleecy wreaths of cloud become arrayed in a crimson glow, which soon floats down its delicate hue to the snowy crests themselves: ῥοδοδάκτυλος Ἠώς has lost none of her classic charms. Presently, while the banks of cloud rolling in the abyss in the foreground are borrowing the rosy tints of their loftier brothers, the rising sun has flashed upon the peaks with a gleam of lurid gold, and in a few moments they have exchanged their golden fringe for an embroidery of rays of dazzling silver, glittering the more brightly from their dark frame of mist. Alas! too often then the watery curtain spreads, and hides in its dismal folds this fairy scene.

Darjeeling itself is situated on a beautiful slope,

and its great elevation gives it a climate which is almost English. Accordingly, the tropical vegetation is not nearly so dense as in the low-lying plains, and it is noticeable that the more hardy firs do not supply its place. The noble Kinchinjanga, on the north, is just outside the borders of Thibet, and between it and Darjeeling lies the district of Sikkim. ruled by a native rajah under our protection. Fifty miles westward is Nepaul, and towards the east are the regions of Bootan and Assam. By rail Darjeeling is 379 miles from Calcutta.

Its inhabitants, apart from a few real Indians, are a very mongrel lot, claiming, we may suppose, some relationship with Thibetans, Bootans, Nepaulese, and various other mountain tribes. They look like an ideal cross between Chinamen and Malays; they are wrapped in dingy clothes, and many of them wear a suspicious-looking cutlass in their girdles. Their shops and houses, like most oriental abodes, have only a ground floor; and in the cold mornings they are to be seen through the entrance comfortably warming themselves over basins of fire.

On the way back from Darjeeling to Siliguri there is ample time to form some general opinion of the Himalayas. They extend everywhere on an overpowering scale, and their brown and timbered slopes blend imperceptibly with the far-reaching chasms, down which the moving train allows a moment's glance. Here and there, too, they are dotted with small white houses, doubtless the homes of tea-planters. The sublimity of the mountains is grand, their Titanic splendour overwhelming; but, if comment on anything so fine is not forbidden, they have about them a slight monotony which is a little apt to detract from their combined magnificence, and they cannot exhibit the furious torrents and fantastic spurs which adorn the Rocky Mountains. Their height also is somewhat lost, as they rise from so high a base; but nevertheless a visit to the Himalayas is by no means a misspent holiday.

Returning to Calcutta, the East Indian Railway starts from there as the recognised highway through Northern India. In twelve hours it passes Patna, historically famous as one of the earliest English trading settlements on the Ganges. It is a considerable town, of dilapidated mud cottages, and it constitutes the capital of Behar.

The country to Benares is very flat, but fertile; and, besides producing bearded wheat and other crops, it is parcelled out in white poppy plantations for opium. The native dresses are very bright and ornamental; so are the many small and beautiful birds, all varieties of which—blue and green, black and white, large kites and green parrots—skim along the fields, or bravely watch the train from the telegraph wires.

A keen interest must seize everyone who for the first time enters Benares, that most holy city of the Hindoos, the pride of antiquity, the immemorial centre of religion, wealth, and industry. No view of it can be more favourable than that from the sacred Ganges, on the deck of a native boat fitted with paddle-wheels, and propelled tread-mill fashion by several coolies. Its innumerable temples are marked by pinnacles, piled up, as it were, out of their own miniatures, which stand out from different levels on the bank, and overlook one another in friendly rivalry. But they are not so large as the pagodas of Southern India. At the foot of these, and running quite a mile along the edge of the river, are no less than forty-seven gháts or flights of steps, built, with the houses behind them, by pious rajahs from all parts of India. On these a busy ceremony repeats itself every morning. Thousands of Hindoos, whether rich or poor, residents or pilgrims, Rajpúts and Mahrattas, purify themselves by bathing in the sacred water, pray to the sun or the Ganges, count their beads, and throw flowers or offerings into the curling stream. Along the bank the Manikaranika temple is venerated as the most sacred of all, and close to the ghát which leads to it, a spot is reserved for the cremation of the dead, before scattering their ashes into the holy river. The next is Sindhia's ghát, whose massive stone temple is gradually sinking into the water, and just beyond, the two minarets of Aurangzeb's Mahomedan mosque are the tallest buildings in the town. This mosque, like another in Benares, is a standing insult to the Hindoos, and was erected by the great Mogul on the site of their old temple of Krishna, and out of its very materials. Of the Hindoo temple near the second mosque, an ancient pillared wall is now the humiliated relic.

Upon closer inspection, the city is a trifle disappointing, owing rather, perhaps, to its very high reputation than to its having any particular fault, for in the narrow shrines and dirty alleys there is much, very much, that is unique and interesting. The Golden Temple, dedicated to Síva, forms a little quadrangle, roofed in by a small central dome and two pinnacles, which are mostly covered with richly-gilded copper plates. A few yards off is the famous and fetid Gyán Kúp, or well of knowledge, overspread with a cloth filled with offerings of flowers, which fall into the well, and add a fresh contribution to its stagnant contents. Among the images and swarms of beggars near the shrines, the bulls and apes lead a frolicking life of luxuriance and sanctity; every whim is humoured, every desire gratified. If a bullock lies down to sleep in a narrow street, it is said that none will dare wake him to get by; if he steals his food from a shop, the owner will rejoice that his merchandise has been devoted to so good a purpose. Many valuables are for sale in the bazaars; the silk embroidery and well-known brass-work are those that best suit a traveller's thirst for curiosities. An obsolete observatory looks down upon the Ganges; and near the cantonment is the Benares government school, where Hindoo day scholars are educated for about four rupees a month.

The palace of the Maharajah of Benares at Ramnagar borders on the river about three miles up from the city, and those who are so fortunate as to have enjoyed his courteous hospitality and the civilities of his genial old councillor, the Rajah Sivaprasád, must ever retain the most pleasing recollections of their visit. The marbles and ivory models in the palace are exquisite; but to be honoured by the Maharajah with an entertainment of Hindoo music and dancing-girls affords precisely that instructive insight into the amusements of upper Hindoo life, which it is sometimes so difficult to obtain. He is a charming old gentleman, very kind, and deservedly popular in Benares, but he is keenly sensitive to his failing sight. The spacious room, into which his guests are ushered, has on such occasions but little furniture—little more than an Indian carpet and a few tables in the corners, besides on one side two rows of chairs to accommodate all the guests and retainers invited. In the front row, among the guests, sits the Maharajah, and his adopted son and grandson, all of them magnificently dressed : just behind is a whole retinue of attendants, and the proceedings are eyed with interest by the servants, who stand round at the sides. The otherwise empty centre of the room is occupied by a royal pigeon dyed crimson with a black tail, which struts about on a small table, and looks very self-important; and the only other disputant of the floor is a hookah, lazily puffed at by the venerable host. If once the luckless bird should venture to stir off his rest, the commotion among the attendants is that of stern and helpless despair. Presently, three musicians squat down before the assembly, and play several plaintive tunes on Hindoo guitars and fiddles, together with plausible variations (for the benefit of English strangers) of ' We won't go home till morning,' ' John Peel,' and other national melodies. When they have finished, two dancing-girls come in, and perform many patient manœuvres. Hindoos never dance themselves, unless quite carried away in the worship of their idols; they leave it all to these professionals, who gesticulate mildly, and twirl, and sing, as they hope best to please their gracious patrons. They are brilliantly dressed in purple and gold, or green and silver, with nose-rings, bangles, and ear-rings, and their songs are accompanied by a small band which stands behind them, and enlivens their audience with the strains of guitars and a drum. On rising to leave, the old Maharajah decorates each of his guests by throwing over their shoulders a ringlet of red and gold cord, and in these splendid ornaments they are conducted to the door of the palace and expected to ride out of the grounds on the Maharajah's elephants. The elephant ride is a high mark of oriental favour. The seats on the elephants' backs are made of wood overlaid with embossed silver, but when each monster is on the point of kneeling down—skilfully, it is true—to let its riders mount and dismount by the help of a ladder, the prospect of the jerk on either occasion almost requires the composure of a Nimrod.

The Maharajah keeps a 'stable' of forty elephants. Eastern greatness is everywhere measured by the number of attendants, servants, and elephants that an owner possesses, and we in England can hardly realise what a blow it would be to British rule in India, if the Viceroy never went on his journeys in more than ordinary state.

No great distance from Benares the old Buddhist remains at Sarnath are a great attraction to antiquarians. Benares and its vicinity have a history in every age, and 600 years before the Christian era, this was the first preaching-place of the retired Prince Buddha. Possibly to commemorate this event, the solid round ruin of brick and stone, now left at Sarnath, was originally commenced; but it was never finished, and its crumbling block of stone is the only existing vestige of its ancient greatness. It is over one hundred feet high, and its lower portion was encompassed by a sculptured girdle of costly designs and leafy patterns, now almost entirely worn away. Above it were eight niches, at even intervals from each other, and apparently intended to support seated Buddhas; and on the inner bricks the private marks of the old masons are still wonderfully well preserved. Maybe, it is 2,000 years old. The ground near it contains many old stones and ruined masonry, but a modern temple of the Jain Buddhists has lately disturbed its solitude. It was successfully excavated in 1836 by General Cunningham.

Taking the westward mail from Benares, Allahabad is the nearest well-known stopping-place, but with the holy city of Benares, it has indeed nothing in common. Just before reaching it, the East Indian Railway crosses the Jumna, upon a magnificent bridge of fourteen arches, and more than half a mile long—one of those immense railway structures so often necessitated by the enormous breadth of Indian rivers. Allahabad derives its present importance from being the capital of the North-West Provinces, and therefore a government metropolis; and its situation at the junction of the yellow Ganges and blue Jumna has been of considerable strategical value. The junction of the rivers can be well seen from the fort, thrown up by the Great Mogul Akbar in A.D. 1575, and now modernised as barracks; but in the dry season the wide expanse of sand somewhat detracts from the effect of their confluence. In the Khusroo Bagh, or public gardens of Allahabad, there are three curious mausoleums.

Cawnpore and Lucknow are chiefly notorious on account of the mutiny, a dark page in Indian history, the reminiscences of which it would be better in some degree to obliterate and ignore. Like other places in India, both of them are straggling towns.

In Cawnpore, the sites of Wyndham's camp and Wheeler's entrenchment, the memorial church with seven mournful tablets on either side of the altar, the Hindoo temple and flight of steps by the Ganges which saw the massacre of Wheeler's garrison by the treacherous Nana Sahib, and finally the Memorial Garden, are all painful recollections of the events of '57. In the last the Government has erected a beautiful marble angel and enclosure over the well, which disclosed in that terrible July so hideous a spectacle to the troops of General Havelock.

Lucknow, on the river Gumtí, was the former capital of Oudh, and is now included in the North-West Provinces. It is the largest city in India next to Calcutta, Madras, and Bombay, and of its population of 275,000, three-fifths are Hindoos. The palaces of Lucknow, and mosques, and domes, and mausoleums, are out-matched elsewhere, and all interest centres in the ruined residency, with its riddled and desolate tower, which recalls its brave defence against an overwhelming force of sepoys. The city encircles it everywhere, and the level position of its surroundings gave every advantage to the attacking rabble of mutineers.

In Wingfield Park the grounds are prettily laid out with flowers and statuettes, and the red pointsettias and bushes of purple bourgainvilliers are very gay companions to the other plants.

Continuing on to Agra, the convenient situation and far-famed loveliness of the Taj Mahal prompts a visit to it without delay; and though most expectations are deceptive, for they always prejudice one's judgment, not even the highest could well be disappointed with this jewel of India. It is a white marble mausoleum, about 240 feet high, built in A.D. 1630 by the Great Mogul, Shah Jehán, in memory of Mumtaz Mahal, his favourite wife. It stands upon an immense white marble platform, 314 feet square, which is raised 18 feet above a platform of red sandstone, with a substructure of chunam, the red sandstone platform being itself six feet above the garden leading to it. Through the garden runs a long narrow pond, 880 feet in length, lined with trees, and divided in the middle by another white marble platform; and at its entrance is a vast and magnificent red sandstone gateway, well-proportioned, and inlaid with marble patterns, all of which would attract the utmost admiration, but for the magnetic vicinity of the Taj beyond.

Of the Taj itself it is hard to write. It stands in peerless loveliness, protected at each corner of its platform by a tall white minaret. Everywhere its dazzling whiteness is almost blinding, and its symmetry it is impossible to overrate. Though it has eight sides, its general appearance is square, and the four low towers or cupolas on its roof strikingly relieve its all-absorbing and graceful dome. The dome is crowned with a crescent and a spike of gilded copper, and wreaths of coloured marble are let in round its base, while, both outside and in, the walls are inlaid with black marble inscriptions of Arabic from the Koran, and flowery designs of agate, bloodstone, cornelian, coral, or lapis lazuli, in themselves quite an exquisite work, and yet so tastefully devised that they only serve to bring out the whiteness of the whole. Near the porch and inside, these designs surround a dado of larger flowers, carved in relief in the white marble, and others add to the beauty of the tombs of Shah Jehán and his wife, which form an appropriate centre to the building immediately under the dome. The emperor's tomb is adorned with an amazing pattern of tiny poppies, each flower of which is only about three-quarters of an inch in size, but is made up of nearly thirty inlaid pieces of agate or cornelian. Round these tombs, or rather cenotaphs—for the real tombs are in a vault below—is a screen about six feet high, which, like all the windows, is a completely perforated lacework of white marble, a labour so unique and wonderful that it alone would be worth many visits. Altogether, the snow-white purity of the Taj has a magic fascination, and every stone of it is a proof of the skill of its unknown architect, and the priceless splendour of the court of the Great Mogul.[1] Its cost is

---

[1] The architect's nationality is claimed alike by Hindoos, Italians, and French.

The Taj; Agra

variously estimated, but much of its construction was doubtless unpaid for. The Jumna, with tortoises revelling on its sandbanks, flows on the north.

By far the best view of the Taj is from the top of its tall red sandstone gateway. Looking down upon the long narrow pond, nothing could be more effective than the two dark bands of trees on each side, which lend their natural freshness to intensify its silvery gleams.

The tomb of I'timádu 'd daulah on the farther side of the Jumna, is one of the most beautiful buildings in Agra, and second only to the Taj. It is the mausoleum of Ghiyás Beg (high treasurer to the emperor Jehangír), of his wife, and others, and is wholly encased in white marble, with a fine cupola at each of the four corners. Taken altogether, it is much smaller than the Taj, but the architecture is equally perfect, and the windows are an exquisite lattice-work of white marble. It is also more profusely inlaid with patterns, and there is more painting, mosaic, and stucco. The tracery round the windows is almost inimitable, —but description as usual is useless.

In the Agra Fort, whose massive red sandstone walls and turrets were originally built by the illustrious Akbar, the Pearl Mosque, and the palaces of Akbar, Jehangír, and Shah Jehán, are left to typify the spectral lustre of those dusky ages, and though the palaces have been sadly mutilated by English and Mahratta soldiers, some of the dining-rooms and assembly-halls are still great marvels of workmanship.

Agra jail is the largest in India, and contains accommodation for about 2,500 prisoners. Last year, however, it only lodged half that number, a decrease possibly to be attributed to the five good previous harvests; and if this assumption is correct, it strongly exemplifies the connection between poverty and crime, and testifies to the advancing comfort of the people. Among the prisoners there are sometimes one or two Europeans. The system which prevails in the jail of employing the better class of prisoners as warders seems an efficient one: and the ordinary prisoners labour mainly at the manufacture of carpets, which fetch high prices in London; while occasionally, out of sheer mischief, they set fire to the whole of their work.

Sikandara, a few miles' drive from Agra, is the mausoleum of Akbar, but at the start the driving in the streets requires some caution, as natives are a capital hand at being run over, and perhaps by way of revenge when you are walking, are equally clever at running over you. It stands in a garden approached by another huge red sandstone gateway, nearly as high and elaborate as that in front of the Taj. The mausoleum consists of a white marble ground floor with several beautiful marble tombs, almost every one having, as it were, a chapel to itself. The first, second, and third floors are pillared terraces of red sandstone; the uppermost is unlike them. It is a kind of square courtyard, unroofed, and surrounded by a colonnade of white marble ten feet wide, and arched windows of white marble lacework, of which most of the panels are differently designed. In the centre, a white marble cenotaph stands over the hero's tomb of the same material in a vault underground. Though of no unusual size, it is quite radiant with intricate Arabian characters intermingled with the minutest of flowery carvings, and at its head a small font-like pillar was once resplendent with the famous Kuh-i-Noor. It makes the grave a fitting resting-place for the buried conqueror.

Futtehpore Sikri, the deserted city of Akbar, is a longer expedition from Agra, twenty-two miles by carriage. This is one of those deserted cities which abound in India, erected at lavish expenditure by some great Mogul (in this case on a spot where no water was to be found), only to be abandoned so soon as his caprice should dictate. Its fine mosque, with corridors of carved pillars, its magnificent gateway, and the royal palace, with separate portions for Akbar's three wives, one Christian, one Mahomedan, and one Hindoo, are all built of the ordinary hard red sandstone to be found in quarries in the neighbourhood. In a red quadrangle, the tomb of his chief priest, the sheik Selim Chistie, is exceedingly handsome; enclosed in a small roof and dome of white marble, with the usual windows of glistening marble trellis-work, and covered with a canopy of mother-of-pearl. Near the gateway is a deep green pond of stagnant water, where the most superhuman courage would scarcely induce one to wash one's hands, but into which very little 'backsheesh' will persuade a native to leap eighty feet, foot-foremost from the top of the palace!

Along the road to Futtehpore is a long low avenue of trees. Camels and donkeys are not uncommon objects: but either bullocks or buffaloes draw most of the carts, and work nearly all the innumerable wells; and a European's amusement may be pardoned when the sacred bullocks are mercilessly flogged. The bearded wheat and barley are flourishing crops;—would indeed that the British farmer could boast of such a quality!— and in the early spring the other produce is mostly lentils and castor-oil, resembling respectively birch underwood and tall hollyhocks. Among the birds the green parrots are predominant.

While at Agra, or elsewhere, it would be a pity to miss such national institutions as the Indian juggler and the Indian snake-charmer. The latter, it is true, is a poor quack, and his performance a feeble one. His cobras, whose fangs have been extracted, rear their hoods as if stupefied by the execrable music, and look foolishly about, following the direction of the instrument; till at last, when they are no longer excited, they coil themselves up, and their hoods subside. A good juggler has certainly some unfathomable tricks. After imprisoning under a basket, in full view of his audience, one live pigeon and four feathers, he can immediately disclose a waddling brood of five full-grown pigeons : he can thrust any sword through a wicker-work case in which a child is sitting without injury to the child : and he can grow a mango-tree in a few minutes from its seed under a coverlet of matting.

CHAPTER VIII.

NORTHERN INDIA: DELHI TO THE KHYBER PASS;
UMRITSUR TO BOMBAY.

RUNNING on westward, the East Indian Railway reaches its terminus at Delhi; the capital of the old Mogul Empire, and the scene of so many vicissitudes. There are three old Delhis, solid deserted ruins, at some distance from the modern city, the Mahomedan name of which is Shahjehanabad, or the city of Shah Jehán. It was founded by that emperor in 1631, and surrounded by him with a wall seven miles in circumference.

The inner fort is entered by the magnificent Lahore Gate, whose red sandstone fortifications are built very like those at Agra, and on its farther side, overlooking the Jumna, are the exquisite remains of the now-mutilated palace of the Mogul emperors. The chief of these is the Diwan-i-Khás or private audience-hall, 90 feet by 70, and 19 feet high, constructed wholly of white marble and open at the sides. It has thirty-two massive white marble pillars, ornamented with gold, and inlaid with patterns of flowers; and in it, on a marble pedestal, formerly stood the famous peacock throne which was carried away to Persia by the odious Nadir Shah. To the north of this building are the imperial baths, and on the south the zenana, all very similar in texture and exceedingly beautiful. Close by they are rivalled by the small Pearl Mosque, entered through a bronze door, which has been executed with intricate tracings; and, not far off it, the Diwan-i-'Am, or public audience-hall, presents an imposing structure. It has three rows of red sandstone pillars, at the back of which are raised the emperor's white marble seat and canopy, both beautifully set and designed, while in the recess behind them flowers and very naturally-drawn green parrots are inlaid into the wall.

Inside the city-wall, by far the most prominent and handsome building is the Jumma Musjid (mosque), from the top of whose noble minarets, 130 feet high, the city of Delhi lies at a spectator's feet. Its three domes are white; the rest is a mixture of white and red, the minarets being striped perpendicularly. In front of it is a large red sandstone quadrangle, enclosed by an open arcade of red pillars, and at each side of the quadrangle a tall gateway faces a stately row of red steps. Nor is the mosque destitute of holy relics. In a remote corner, under the jealous guardianship of an aged priest, are some old Koran manuscripts, Mahomet's slipper, his footprint on a stone, and a hair of his moustache.

In the Chandni Chauk, or Piccadilly of Delhi, where the shops of the native goldsmiths and the depôts of Cashmere shawls soon allure the reckless tourist, stands a small mosque with three golden domes, from which in 1739 Nadir Shah watched the sack of Delhi and the atrocities of his barbarous soldiers. The streets are thronged with irrepressible merchants, who pester one's carriage with their solicitations and cards of advertisement; and the many dancing-girls are equally pushing to make their songs and music a pretext for a general blockade.

It was the low Ridge to the north-west of Delhi that played so leading a part during the mutiny, and formed the base of our operations in besieging the rebels, who had then seized the fortifications. Higher than the surrounding plain, it overlooks the minarets and palaces of the city, and the Jumna flowing by its side; and shows glimpses of the thick masonry of Shah Jehán, where the ruined bastions, and trench, and gates, and terraces still seem fresh from their breach by our gallant brigades. The Mori bastion, with ramparts so formidable that we found them hard to silence, faces the twin arches of the Cashmere gate, whose doors were dislodged by the self-sacrifice of a very heroic little band. Under a constant stream of shot and shell, and accompanied only by a dozen English and native soldiers, Lieuts. Home and Salkeld dragged up to the gate several bags of powder, and there exploded them to effect an entrance, which was quickly followed up by a column of the troops. At the same time another column, animated by the courage of General Nicholson, scaled the breaches near the gate, and rushed through into the town; but they were fated, at the moment of victory, to lose their noble leader, while endeavouring to storm a narrow street. He is buried in the Delhi cemetery, where a simple railing and inscription call attention to his tomb. The capture of Delhi was the death-blow of the mutiny, and restored once more the equity of British rule.

Upon the crest of the Ridge the head-quarters of our cantonment are represented by Flagstaff Tower, now a ruin, and Hindoo Rao's house, which belonged to that celebrity of the day. Near it an old pillar is inscribed with the edicts of King Asoka, issued by him about B.C. 250. It is one of several which he erected in India, and others of them are still extant. Beyond the Ridge the plains sparkled with all the pomp and ceremony of an Eastern *tomásha*, when at the Imperial assemblage in 1877 the Queen was proclaimed Empress of India.

Several high-domed tombs, of the usual type, have solemnised the environs of Delhi. Among these that of the Emperor Humáyun, the father of Akbar, was the refuge of the last king of Delhi while the city was being besieged and stormed in 1857, till finally he was traced there by the English, and arrested in the very passages of the tomb.

But by far the most remarkable structure in this neighbourhood is the celebrated and singular Kutub Minár, eleven miles away from the present city, and mounting up skyward on the site of one of those old Delhis, all three of which are now roofless and deserted It was probably the attempted consummation of some prodigious dream, such as often pervaded the brain of oriental despots. Extortionate in their taxation, unscrupulous in its expenditure, they sought to raise some personal memorial, which might overcome the shortness of human memories, and proclaim their magnificence to all posterity. The pyramids have fulfilled the intention of their founders; Kutub has been equally successful in his minár. What it is, is not easy to explain—except by negatives, for its shape is peculiarly its own. It is not exactly a

Kutub Minár, near Delhi

tower, nor a minaret, nor a column, nor a monument, nor a pillar, yet it claims relationship to them all: it is 240 feet high, contains a winding staircase of 379 steps, and is said to have been completed about A.D. 1220. Its five portions of red sandstone and grey rock taper upwards with strict geometrical accuracy, very strikingly, each being smaller than the last, and separated from it by a balcony. They are all perpendicularly grooved, and inscribed near the balconies with ornamental bands of Arabian characters, alas! no longer very legible. At the foot of the edifice are the remains and gateways of a handsome old mosque (Kutbu 'l Islam), itself built upon the ruins of a Hindoo temple, whose archways have once been very grand, and whose carved pillars seem now to be miniatures of those in Southern India. Near by there is also a curious iron pillar, a large tomb of an emperor called Altamsh, and the deserted stump of a minár, which was actually intended to be twice the size of the Kutub. Besides these, a few more marble tombs and heaps of ruined walls alone represent this old Delhi; and among them one or two wells give the natives an opportunity, for a few annas, of jumping down them eighty feet. Another old Delhi stands five miles east of the Kutub at Tughlakabad.

Modern Delhi is a pretty town, with young

avenues along its drives and streets. For administrative purposes it has been in the Punjaub since the mutiny, to weaken its political importance, though historically and geographically it does not belong to it. It contains surprisingly few Europeans; and its native population is about half Mahomedan and half Hindoo. Their food is mostly millet—rice would be rather a luxury; and in the early year, until the ripening in April of the delicious and abundant mangoes, few fruits are available except indifferent oranges and unusually soapy bananas. But tropical fruits in general are very tasteless. Up to March the climate of Northern India is charming in the daytime, though the nights are in comparison incredibly cold.

At the risk of rheumatic consequences, it is well to be provided against the change of temperature upon going northwards to Lahore, for Punjaub colds are proverbially more incurable and troublesome than others. Nor is the coolness the only warning of the altered state of circumstances; to be again in a land of deciduous trees is indeed an inclement anomaly, to which at first it is not easy to accustom oneself. The Punjaub, too, is the land of the Sikhs; and their manly bearing, as they stand erect among the saunterers on the railway platforms, does full justice to their martial figures.

Lahore, the capital of the Punjaub, is like

other Indian cities in covering a large area, and it is divided into a European and a native quarter. In the European quarter there is a museum of curious local productions, a red brick cathedral, the law courts, and a jail which manufactures first-rate Indian carpets. Montgomery Hall is a public reading-room, and on gay occasions is used for balls. There are also several modernised buildings, which, like Government House itself, are the converted tombs or mausoleums of ancient Mahomedan dignitaries! The usual round of the native quarter—partly, perhaps, performed on an elephant—includes a small golden-domed mosque and the large Jumma Musjid, one of red sandstone and white marble. But the best buildings are the Vazir Khan mosque, whose square walls and corner minarets are largely covered with coloured tiles; the tomb of the great Runjeet Singh, made of chunam and white marble handsomely inlaid; and the Fort, with its palace of mirrors and small armoury of Sikh weapons. There is in it a good deal of the beautiful white marble-work, so inexhaustible at Agra and Delhi; but unless gifted with very great talent for architectural detail, it is possible to have enough, even of that!

Just beyond the river Ravee, and five miles from Lahore, the tomb of the Emperor Jehangír is situated at Shádara, amid porticoes and gateways and minarets; and, after the fashion of his father Akbar's tomb at Sikandara, it is approached through an extensive garden, very neatly preserved by native gardeners.

The Sikhs have a religion of their own, with copious extracts both from Hindooism and Buddhism; and a prophet of their own. A few of them cherish a simmering dislike to British rule, and a desire for independent sovereignty, although this would indefinitely increase their taxation; but it is not unreasonable to suppose that the real root of their discontent lies in their having at present to tolerate the Mahomedans, whereas they would prefer to thrash them. There seems to be no movement in favour of the Maharajah Dhuleep Singh's return; on the contrary, the intrigues are confined to *him*.

The train onwards from Lahore to Peshawur is a very slow one. It stops at Rawul Pindi, a name now quite familiar from the telegrams in the newspapers, and crosses the Indus over Attock Bridge. On swerving round to the north, it is then directly separated by the river from Attock town, with its crumbling fortifications and defences, which were built, doubtless, by the Sikhs against Afghans; but the Indus here is a comparatively small, though rapid stream. The land is partially cultivated, but generally very sterile; and it is sometimes fantastically broken by deep and dried-up watercourses, or waste, stony hills.

From the old Peshawur fort there is a pretty view of the Peshawur plain, edged by the snowy tips and brown mountains which converge towards the west into the Khyber Pass, and are altogether not unlike the plains of Lombardy. To the south-east lies the town. The fort itself is an ancient building of mud walls, impressive, it seems, to the natives, and useful as barracks for some of our troops; but it would probably totter to its very foundations rather than discharge heavy guns at an enemy. In the town the houses are chiefly built of mud, one or two storeys high, and the roofs, also of mud, are perfectly flat. Among modern edifices the native Christian church is the most interesting. It is built in eastern architecture, with texts in Persian outside, and the font inside is constructed for total immersion, and is lined with a white marble rim, engraved with Persian characters in black. The trade and workmanship of the district are very primitive and rough; one peculiar industry is that of designing patterns in wax upon cloth. Besides this, business is done in carpets, pottery, tin and black copper work, and furs, for which the neighbourhood is more or less famous; and the many peach plantations produce fairly good fruit.

An invitation to tea from a native Peshawuri gentleman is a civility not easily to be forgotten. He provides, as he would for his own friends, cups of green tea, flavoured with cloves and other spices, sugar, but no milk. Instead of bread and butter, he hands round excellent white Cábul grapes, and well-packed strawberry-baskets of Cábul apples, though the apples, it must be admitted, are very hard and tasteless. Nearer Herat, it is usual, when you are calling upon your friends, to take two cups of tea; and if you ask for a third cup, it is understood that you wish to be off; but if your host pours you out a third, he is politely hinting that he has had enough of you. What an ideal society to live in!

Peshawur is really quite unlike an Indian village, and indeed, it is a mere conventionality to call it in India at all. Its population of 58,000 contains 49,000 Mahomedans, and includes very many races or nationalities. Sikhs, Punjaubies,[1] Peshawuries, Afreedies, and Afghans are all there; the men often clothed in dirty white dresses and turbans, occasionally varied with a daub of colour; the younger women altogether veiled in white. Many of the faces look exceedingly sullen and brutal; there are endless blood-feuds, and frequent

[1] All Sikhs are strictly, of course, Punjaubies; but the term 'Punjaubi' is generally applied to Punjaub Mahomedans.

robberies, and evidence is so difficult that the commissioner is empowered to convict an accused person at his discretion without it. It is not hard to believe that between 80 and 120 murders are committed there a year, and that there is a standing gallows.

And now to set out for the Khyber Pass. The first ten miles to Jamrood Fort lie along the plains; but about half-way, a mud police-station situated on an abrupt line where every sign of cultivation vanishes, marks the strict termination of British ground. Here begins the independent territory, which extends to the further side of the Khyber under the precarious dominion of six Afreedi mountain tribes, the main road alone being kept indirectly under our protection. At this point it is flat, stony land, and the mud fort of Jamrood, which, as it is approached, much resembles a turret-ship, seems a British oasis in its midst. The fort is without cannon, by treaty obligation; were it otherwise, possibly its mud walls would not stand their recoil. It now becomes necessary to take horses, and to be escorted through the pass by mounted Afreedies; whereupon, sometimes, on leaving the fort, our drilling regiments of Afreedi recruits will speed the parting traveller with a lusty salute on bagpipes and drums. They are piping Afreedi love-songs, in the good old

European spirit of knight-errantry, and conclude with—what needs at the moment quite as much explanation—a flourish for 'God save the Queen'! Four miles more bring the road to the Khyber's mouth, flanked at a distance on each side by several Afreedi towers, incessantly bent upon firing at each other, unless they have put up white stones to betoken a momentary truce. Often our telegraph-wire through the Pass is stolen, as it cuts up neatly into slugs or bullets, which are always serviceable to defray the cost of some family feud; but such outrages we punish by a heavy fine.[1] The entrance to the Pass, like the rest of it, is absolutely barren; everywhere sterile, steep, and rocky hills more or less closely follow the winding road, and lend themselves admirably to the barbarian war-practice of rolling down great stones from the top, which was such an annoyance to our native troops during the campaign of 1878. Here and there we have built small towers to protect the road, and these are garrisoned by Afreedies in our pay; but trees and vegetation are altogether wanting. About three miles on are the Shagei heights, a wider expanse of high and undulating ground, surrounded by the desolate hills, and about three miles away from the fort of Ali

[1] See p. 173 *inf*.

Musjid. It was from the Shagei heights that Sir Frederick Roberts attacked Ali Musjid in 1878, and eventually stormed its commanding position; and as the Afghans had previously deemed it impregnable, its capture was of great consequence to the success of our arms. It stands on a well-chosen eminence, about 3,000 feet above the sea, and 4,000 feet below the encircling peaks, and almost blocks the narrow defile in the Pass; yet the stream of water tainted with antimony at its foot, and the biting winds which continually blow up the valley, make it a most unhealthy residence even for the Afreedies themselves. Though the British Government has patched it up, it is still a good type of a primeval Afghan fort, built of rough stons and lined inside with mud-work; but it would not be politic at present to entrust any cannon to the few Afreedi mercenaries who are stationed there, and indeed their adherence to us in case of war could scarcely be counted upon after any serious reverse. On the other hand, if we are the victors, as we ought to be, they are an appreciable power. By arrangement with the wild marauders,—the best that could be made under the circumstances,—it is only on Tuesdays and Fridays that travellers and convoys from Peshawur can safely enter the Pass. Accordingly, on those days, that end of it is all astir with the two caravans of several hundred camels and many Afghan followers, going to and from Cábul and Peshawur, on the journey of about 170 miles, which they accomplish in ten or twelve days. They give a great reality to the scene; and the caravans to Cábul are heavily laden with tea, stones, and other materials, besides (just recently) large iron pipes destined for the new waterworks of the Ameer. These latter are transported one on each side of a camel, and are rather formidable weapons to a rider's knees, if a crowd of stupid animals should come brushing up against him. From Ali Musjid to the further end of the Khyber near Lundi Kotal is a distance of about seventeen miles.

The Khyber is one of the three great passes which traverse the nameless ranges of mountains between India and Afghanistan. The other two are the Gomul Pass, and, in Beluchistan, the Bolan Pass, the latter not therefore in India at all. Among the smaller passes are the Hernai, through which a railway of rapid curves and gradients has lately been engineered to secure a second route to Quetta, and the Kohat Pass.

The Afreedies are fine-looking men, of a much lighter colour than the Indians, and some of them seem far too merry to be suspected of treachery or ill-nature. Others, however, look decidedly less sincere. We pay to the six Afreedi tribes 80,000 rupees a year in consideration of our receiving the tolls through the pass which they formerly appropriated, amounting at the present time to about 65,000 rupees a year, although we could double them were it our policy to do so. In addition, we pay 100,000 rupees a year to the Afreedi fighting men, on condition that they keep the road clear, which is a very substantial return; and if a murder takes place upon it, or the telegraph wire is stolen, &c., we can punish them by cutting down their allowance in proportion to the offence. Three hundred rupees is the usual fine inflicted for a murdered man, and the sum is found to be sufficiently preventive. The system is an ingenious one and answers well.

Those who enlist as our mercenaries provide themselves with arms and uniforms. They are dressed in a neat sandy-coloured tunic, hardly distinguishable from the colour of the mountains, and relieved with red; their Snider rifles are presumably stolen. Each man receives as wages nine rupees a month, or two rupees a month more than is given to an ordinary sepoy.

That the control of the Khyber Pass may guide the course of future events is a political certainty, and this is not the place to consider in detail the contingencies of the problem, or the anxieties of Russia to obtain a port in the Persian Gulf. But if the Russians advance to Herat, we *must* take Candahar, if only in deference to public opinion both here and in India, especially in India among the natives; and, should war subsequently ensue, the Ameer will wisely wait to take the winning side. In any case, however—and war is clearly no necessity—a railway through Afghanistan is but a matter of time, which may spontaneously lead to a division of the country between the Russians and ourselves, and thus impose upon both parties a very unenviable dominion over the treacherous Afghans. The railway is now completed on our side as far as Chaman, a hundred miles beyond Quetta, and on the Russian side to Merv, from which before long it will be extended to Penjdeh. We must never forget that the possession of our Indian Empire transforms us into a continental military power, and makes us liable at any moment to continental hostilities.

But time presses on, and compels rapid strides to Bombay. Bidding farewell to Peshawur, it is necessary to return again through Lahore to Delhi, crossing the five rivers of the Punjaub, and stopping, if convenient, to break the journey at Umritsur.[1] This town is celebrated for the Golden

[1] Or Amritsar. The spelling of Indian names is provokingly changeable. It requires some talent to appreciate such cyphers as Kahnpur or Lacknau, instead of the good old forms, Cawnpore and Lucknow.

Temple of the Sikhs, and is the head-quarters of their religion. The temple stands in the middle of a tank or pond, and is at first sight half hidden by a hideous Gothic clock-tower of red brick, which is a sheer piece of British vandalism. Its architecture, a mixture between Hindoo and Mahomedan, is not exactly beautiful; but it is almost entirely covered with plates of copper gilt, which form an effective coating, and they are elaborately embossed inside. Unlike most temples, it has a first floor, and there is also a good deal of painting on the chunam or stucco walls. On the ground floor a seated priest daily intones a few verses of the Sikh bible, and is listened to by a squatting semi-circular audience, who sit round a red cloth spread out in the midst of them for offerings of cowries to the temple. From twenty to fifty large cowries are the equivalent of one pie, and as 192 pice go to one rupee, it wants many cowries to make up a good offertory. The entrance to the temple is along a black and white marble pier facing the two gates of life and immortality. The backs of the wooden doors on the gate of life are superbly inlaid with ivory; at the gate of immortality baptisms are performed. A man to be baptized into the brotherhood of Sikhs is first required to repeat an orthodox catechism. A small iron dagger is then placed in his turban, and this, like the iron bracelets commonly worn by many Sikhs, is esteemed to be a token of valour. Water is next sprinkled over his face, and the ceremony ends by his attending to a brief exhortation from the priest, which includes the excellent advice that he should obey the government and be foremost in battle. The awful weapons of the early Sikh prophets are treasured up close by.

Travelling on to Delhi, a change has there to be made on to the narrow-gauged Rajputana-Malwa railway, which has its southern terminus at Ahmedabad. This particular narrow gauge is a serious hitch in the Indian railway system, and might cause a very critical delay in the hurried transportation of troops, as it forms part of the direct line between Bombay, and Delhi, Calcutta, or Peshawur: and it is therefore much to be desired that means will soon be found to remedy this defect.

One of the most interesting cities through which it runs is Jeypore, a capital of Rajputana. Its interest lies emphatically in its Rajpút people, whose conscious pride scarcely yields to that of the Nizam's subjects in Hyderabad, and whose upright walk and independent demeanour stamp them all over as the inhabitants of a real native state. The city proper, founded by the Maharajah Sawai Jey Singh in 1728, is marked out by its wall, and his wisdom in choosing a site has fortified it with hills everywhere but on the south-west. It has very neat houses, generally painted a dull red and white, rather Italian in look, and, indeed, rumoured to be the work of an Italian architect; its good roads and wide streets are remarkable, and it even possesses tramways and gas. Hindooism is rampant, and the bullock more sacred than ever, so that even at the British resident's house beef is never an item of the bill of fare. Peacocks are also sacred. There are plenty of them, and they are said to be useful in destroying snakes; and the humane regard of the Hindoos for animal life has overrun the city with pigeons and worthless, drowsy dogs.

Near a palace of the Maharajah's are kept his tigers, his tame alligators and tortoises, lounging away their gluttonous existence in a large tank, and his stable of two hundred Arabian, Indian, and other horses, which frisk about in their daily exercise at a sort of circus-training, full of clever tricks and dances. Just outside the city wall the cenotaphs of the Maharajahs are exquisitely carved with pictures of Hindoo mythology: but there are no tombs, as Hindoo bodies are always cremated, and their ashes committed to the Ganges.

The Maharajah of Jeypore has another palace

at the deserted capital of Ambér, five miles from the city. It stands in a winding valley, and is especially pretty for its situation and charming for its views. At the village of Ghat, only two miles from Jeypore, he also owns a house and garden, and the Ghat valley is very popular with native picnic parties out for a holiday, although wild tigers and leopards roam about the hills at night-time.

The government is superintended by the English resident, who exercises at discretion a power of interference ; and is administered by the Maharajah, or rather his prime minister, with a kind of cabinet council. Out of his large income derived from land revenue, customs, &c. (for Jeypore is a wealthy native state), the Maharajah maintains his army, judiciary, police, public college, gasworks, waterworks, and other public expenses, and provides for his own private wants, the arrangement being closely analogous to our extinct civil list. His army consists of 10,000 or 12,000 men, all told, and he manufactures his own field-pieces, but imports his rifles from England. Altogether the native government is a very creditable one, and gives very general satisfaction, but it would be idle to expect its subordinate officers to be quite proof against bribes.

The Maharajahs of native states such as Jeypore, Jhodpore, and Oodeypore, and especially

Indore, are, of course, persons of greater authority than other more titular maharajahs in India.

Between Jeypore and Bombay the ruined Jain (Buddhist) temples on Mount Aboo usually occupy a two days' excursion, their tracery and carving being considered among the rarest of ancient Indian design. South of these, the railway enter the tropics before running into Ahmedabad, and between this town and Bombay its carriages are insufferably dusty, and greatly disturb one's equanimity in watching the manœuvres of the monkeys, kites, or vultures which sit among the trees along the line.

Once at Bombay, and the traveller is again in view of the ocean. The city is prettily placed, with fine buildings, which are more compact and more metropolis-like than those of either Calcutta or Madras. It is the natural harbour of Western India, and if it were only a little more central and a little farther north (possibly rather big 'ifs'), it would make an ideal capital for the Empire. The native houses are mostly plaster, ornamented with balconies; the market is characteristic and, of its kind, very universal. The fashionable and popular Yacht Club, where a band plays every other evening, has a picturesque look-out over the harbour, and on the opposite side of a bay, five miles by land from the town, and more or less separated from it by groves of cocoa-nut palms, Government House enjoys the sea-breezes of Malabar Point. Its temperature, in consequence, is several degrees cooler than that of the town.

The two sights of Bombay are the Parsee 'Towers of Silence,' and the caves of Elephanta. The Parsees or fire-worshippers are very numerous in Bombay. Their creed embraces belief in a Creator and in a future world, but they also worship the sun and fire, because they hold them to be an earthly personification or manifestation of Him. Their so-called Towers of Silence, half-hidden in a bushy garden, occupy one of the prettiest and most advantageous hills in the neighbourhood, and the fire-temple in the garden is used on the occasion of every funeral, though no one may enter it except Parsees. There are five large towers; each is round, whitewashed, about 150 feet in circumference, and perhaps 20 or 30 feet high, and on their edge, or perched on the palms around them, are at least three hundred morbid-looking vultures. The healthiness of the whole system has been questioned, particularly during an epidemic, when the increased mortality among the large population of Parsees might prove an irremediable difficulty.

The caves of Elephanta are on an island seven and a half miles from the town, but inside the magnificent harbour. They are the wonderful remains of a Hindoo temple, at least a thousand years old, and divide into three portions, entirely excavated out of the solid rock, but the huge idols hewn out against the back walls were much spoilt by the Portuguese at the time when they were masters of the country. The massive, partly fluted pillars have also been shamefully ill-treated, yet they all still present the most curious relics of primeval sculpture, and are very interesting of their kind. Elephanta Island abounds with snakes.

Before taking leave of India, there are two Hindoo ceremonies which it would be a misfortune not to see. One is a Hindoo wedding; the other the festivities of an Indian zemindár or landholder on the birth of a son. The latter is a noisy entertainment, continued daily for about a fortnight, in which dancing-girls, clowns, and jokers emulate each other in their varied accomplishments. The gaieties must be very costly, and must go far to drain the resources of every native gentleman; but they are customary, and therefore cannot be abandoned without incurring the danger of being 'cut' by society:—even the Indians are slaves to the follies of etiquette. A fashionable Hindoo marriage is a gorgeous spectacle. The house and garden are brightly illuminated with festoons of tiny oil lamps, through which the bridegroom arrives about dusk, mounted on horseback, and accompanied by a princely train. On entering the house he is led to a red cushion, prepared for him on the floor, and placed opposite another one which his veiled bride is soon expected to occupy; while on either side two other cushions complete the square, and are reserved for the family relations and the Brahmin priests. Everything is in full view of the rows of native guests sitting in chairs close by, and Europeans are now privileged to peep over from a gallery above. The ceremony is conducted in a mysterious undertone, during which the bridegroom and his still muffled bride are united by a cord of worsted thrown round their necks, the marriage tie being further cemented by joining their hands under a muslin coverlet. Afterwards, at a sort of reception, the guests see much more of the bride than has her husband himself, for in his presence, both before and at the marriage, she is always veiled: and, finally, on their departure, they are all honoured with wreaths of flowers to put over their shoulders, and cocoa-nuts wrapped in gold-leaf, as omens of good luck. The bride and bridegroom would be old enough to be married if their ages were respectively twelve and seventeen, and these deplorably early marriages are largely due to the religious superstition of the Hindoos, who fancy that the chances of their soul's happiness after death are much diminished if their burial rites are not performed by their own male descendants. In Rajputana, however, last spring (1888), the native princes took measures to alleviate this evil by prohibiting the marriage of boys under eighteen, and girls under fourteen; a very commendable step in face of the lively prejudice which it might have excited.

Any concluding remarks about India, which is brimful of interest and treasures, though scarcely at this moment quite equal to Japan, can only be inserted here in the form of very disjointed notes, intended to suggest some of many omissions. It is impossible in a few weeks to master the characteristics of all the races of India; it would be more likely to take a few years to acquire the customs of one. Before travelling in the country, few people have any idea of its vast extent; its empire is a combination of sovereignties; its history comprises the ravages of countless tribes. And in the next place, Eastern and Western minds will not mix: we cannot grasp things from an oriental point of view, but nearly always grope about ingenuously on the one side or the other; and orientals seldom succeed in understanding us.[1]

---

[1] For instance, Indian natives would naturally infer that

Some critics say that we ought to associate more completely with them; but they, at least, do not expect it of us; for the English, like the Mahomedans of old, are looked upon as holding the 'raj,' or rule, for the time being, and, according to Eastern usage, would unquestionably stand aloof.

European commissioners and native officials alike call attention to the general contentment of the people, who are everywhere far happier under our protection than they would be under the unbridled extortions of their own princes. They certainly appear contented and happy; and it is only a *reductio ad absurdum* of sentimental opinion that shows any anxiety to lament their want of boots and shoes. To use the criticism of a native prince, What an idiosyncrasy! There are no poor-houses, for food and charity are cheap and universal; and there are no real grievances, Bengalee baboos generally concocting those that exist, to air their 'learned lumber' in the press.

The recent Indian National Congress is, to a great extent, their creature, and a prototype of the representative institutions for which they have so loudly clamoured. Though its present members

---

England was more powerful than Russia because the Duke of Edinburgh had married the Czar's daughter. Had the Queen's daughter married the Czar's son, their conclusion would have been the other way. And this case is no imaginary exaggeration.

boast of their representative character, they are really self elected from the different districts, and it is clear that their debating assembly has at least an ulterior aim of transferring power to an irresponsible section, which is chiefly composed of native and self-important graduates from our Indian universities. Democracy is a capricious plant, nurtured in the atmosphere of the West; it is quite unfitted for India, and its extensive reproduction there, even should it ever become acclimatised to the country, is still immeasurably distant. It is entirely at variance with the religious creed of the Hindoos; and the adamantine barriers of religion, of race, and caste, which stand in its way, must very long delay its approach.

The obliteration of caste and of the ignominious degradation of women, whose education would work miracles, will be a very slow process. It is the personal interest of the Brahmans to keep caste up, and as the Hindoo priesthood is chosen out of their order alone, they can control the national development within a web of religious superstition. Both the existence of caste among the Hindoos, and their bitter antagonism to the Mahomedans (which is excited to the highest pitch when their religious festivals fall in the same week), have given great opportunities to prove the impartiality of our rule.

It has been our policy to encourage education generally, and some foreigners—the Dutch especially—have been struck with the boldness and dangerous nature of a system, which leads, as they think, along the path towards independence. The Bengalee baboo, just fledged from Calcutta university, has already been referred to as the author of mischievous articles in the vernacular newspapers —mischievous, because they are clever and inexperienced, such as readily mislead the ignorant native. Education has its risks, no doubt; but the Hindoo is no fool, and judicious teaching is at all times less harmful than the eccentricities of untaught ability. Many Hindoos, indeed, have a higher intellect, and apply it far more studiously than many of us at home; but it is in the ordinary practical work, which requires common sense, initiative energy, or presence of mind, that they sink into impenetrable helplessness. They are quite destitute of any genius for organisation, and could never govern themselves advantageously for a very long time to come. It is this side of their nature which tempts the British tourist to treat them with that ill-advised contempt, too readily improved upon by the British officer when he soundly kicks them for such trifles as not talking English. This behaviour, alas! has a very plain analogy to England's bygone treatment of Ireland,

and it would surely be prudent to prevent the possibility of a like result by exercising a little forbearance in time.

Of Christian missions it would be incorrect to speak very disparagingly. But a successful missionary must have the qualities of discretion, firmness, and breadth of view in a very pre-eminent degree, and at present our converts are chiefly drawn from ignorant peasants and artisans, the least influential Mahomedans and the lowest caste of Hindoos.

A few facts about Indian incomes and wages will not be misplaced. A native Indian is considered a rich man if he has command over a lakh of rupees (10,000*l.*, with rupee at 2*s.*); but according to Eastern custom much of this sum is spent upon his poor relations, who are almost wholly dependent upon him. The income of a well-to-do native gentleman would be about 10,000 to 15,000 rupees a year (1,000*l.* to 1,500*l.*). His family expenses would probably amount to some 6,000 rupees a year (600*l.*), and his servants each receive about 60 rupees a year (6*l.*). An ordinary labourer, brass-worker, &c., is paid throughout India about 2 annas a day for unskilled labour; the wages of a skilled labourer may amount to 5 annas a day, or not much more than 5*d.* at the present low rate of exchange.

This broaches upon a topic, the depreciation of the rupee, or, rather, the appreciation of gold, which we cannot be so bold as to discuss at any length, though it is so sore a subject with every Anglo-Indian.[1] It may be observed, however, that as, in India, the purchasing power of the rupee remains the same as it was before its so-called depreciation, *native* officials will work for the same salaries as they then received, and likewise the wages of the *native* labourer have not been affected by its diminished value. Since, therefore, the labourer's productions command in foreign markets the same (gold-standard) price as they did before silver was depreciated, the employer will make an additional profit, in proportion to the difference between the former full value and the present diminished value of the rupee, which will go to improve his plant or working capital, and thus increase the total amount of production. This result must necessarily stimulate the prosperity and trade of India. It can hardly, also, be disputed that if a gold currency did exist, the extraordinary habits of the natives would prompt them to hide a large percentage of it in the ground, so that they would enormously aggravate the evil by causing a still greater demand for the more precious metal.

[1] Silver began depreciating in 1872.

CHAPTER IX.

HOMEWARDS THROUGH ADEN, CAIRO, AND ALEXANDRIA.

SWEEPING out from the fine harbour of Bombay, the homeward mail wends its way to the open sea, bound viâ Aden and Suez. The reminiscences of a P. and O. journey would furnish a volume in themselves. Foremost on deck stands the sporting major, full of anecdotes of tigers, and elephants, and boars, and snipe, thrilling adventures and hairbreadth escapes, anticipations realised or disappointed. Next to him, among other passengers, come the hospitable Indian civilian, returning home once more to the vicissitudes of a cloudy sky; the country clergyman, having enjoyed a three months' holiday in the tropics; or busy city men, travelling with an eye to business, and not a little irritated by the noisy children, whose lungs are a sort of barometer of the state of the sea. There are, too, the chattering busybody, curious about everything but what concerns himself, and perhaps irrepressibly sociable to all his victims in the ship; the Yankee, who has seen everything, and has been contemplating how much water-power could be extracted from the most romantic streams; the Frenchman, communicative of his misgivings about himself, his friends, and the political chaos of his country; the studious German, turning to good account the natural idleness of life at sea; and finally the pensive author, sedulously picking up materials for his intended novel, and always on the look-out for some poignant story. And is there no room for the disdainful cynic, who ridicules his own philosophy, and laughs in his sleeve at the hobbies and absurdities of all his versatile comrades?

The nights are long, the days monotonous. Sometimes a lively genius gets up a game of bull; sometimes the ship runs through a shoal of dolphins, jelly-fish, or porpoises; and occasionally, before navigating dangerous waters, the captain tries his compass, and startles his passengers by whirling the steamer round at an amazing speed. Comic songs or dancing cheer up the evening; and over the edge of the ship the phosphorescence in the sea-foam glimmers by freaks and starts, while skyward the Southern Cross is indeed a sorry fraud.

The following engineering technicalities are not out of place. Going at 14 knots an hour in a calm sea, a steamer of 4,700 tons, drawing 24 feet of water, and fitted with two-cylinder engines, burns 65 to 70 tons of coal a day—coal at Bombay costing 36 shillings a ton. Were it to steam only 13 knots, it would under similar circumstances, burn about 56 tons a day; but the ratio between the increase of speed and the amount of coal consumed is affected by so many causes (*e.g.*, wind, rough sea, currents, depth of ship in water), that it is impossible to reduce its fluctuations to any definite rule. Steamers with the new triple [cylinder] expansion engines economise 18 per cent. of coal over those fitted with the older two-cylinder engines: all steamers, also, naturally burn less coal when they draw less water; but a steamer which draws more water usually compensates for the excess of coal which it consumes by being able to carry an additional cargo. Some of the transatlantic steamers burn nearly 200 tons of coal a day.

About five days after leaving Bombay, the mail anchors off Aden, amid a crowd of nigger-boys, who are paddling about in canoes hollowed out of tree-trunks, and are all ready to dive for whatever money may be thrown to them, regardless of the sharks in the harbour. Only three hours are allowed before making a fresh start, and if the stop happens to come towards evening, the temperature on shore is often much pleasanter than might have been apprehended. There is just time to drive round five miles to the town, up to its water-tanks, and back by the artificial tunnels through the rock leading to the isthmus. The approach to Aden makes a fine picture, its weird serrated outline rising sternly from the sea; but on landing it does not bear a close inspection, and the grim volcanic rock, with scarcely a trace of green, turns out to be nothing better than an accumulated ash-heap. It certainly does not look an inviting abode, though people who have lived there sometimes have an affection for it. The town, with its mixed Arab and negro population, inhabiting their low houses of rough whitewashed stone, is built in the middle of the extinct crater, and its twenty curious concrete tanks, which adapt themselves to the shape of the rock, always make a good pretext for the drive. They collect the heavy rain which is reputed to fall upon the heights only once in three years; and, needless to say, therefore, the tank-water has usually the consistency of pea-soup, and is drinkable only by natives and gardens; the water for the English regiment being always condensed. The underground tunnels, blasted through rock, are also a wonderful work, and connect and strengthen the fortifications.

England took possession of Aden in 1839. It is a part of Bombay presidency, and the general in command also acts as civil governor.

A short four days through the desert blasts of the Red Sea, bring the steamer to Shadwán Island, at the mouth of the Gulf of Suez, a gulf about two hundred miles long, and edged by barren mountains and sandy wastes, evidently more delightful to look at than to live on. At Suez itself, there is unavoidably some delay before entering the canal, in order to arm the ship with a proper pilot, an enlarged rudder, and, at night time, a powerful electric light on its bows.

It is certainly a satisfaction to realise, to sail into for the first time, the great canal. This masterpiece of M. de Lesseps is just 92 miles long, about 27 feet deep, and has, at a guess, an average width of 40 yards, buoys in many places marking the channel for larger ships. As the crow flies, the isthmus here is 72 miles wide, and the mean level of the Red Sea is only 6 inches higher than that of the Mediterranean. Like on a single line of railway, there are stations or *gares* (Fr.) at certain intervals, where ships can pass each other, and where flag signals show their pilots that the canal is unblocked up to the next *gare*. A telegraph wire is laid along the whole distance, and not far from the maritime canal, the Sweet (or

o

fresh) Water Canal supplies Nile water to Suez and the *gares*. The country is a dreary waste of sand, and the sandy banks are constantly slipping or being washed into the canal, so that, despite the small scrub or stony fences to keep them back, it is perpetually in need of dredging. It cost 17,250,000*l.*, and its receipts are now over 2,000,000*l.* a month, 15 per cent. of which is paid to the Egyptian Government. Three-quarters of the tonnage passing through is English, and the dues are very heavy. For instance, the passage of a ship of 5,000 tons once through the canal costs nearly 1,300*l.*, and of this expenditure a small item is 8*s.* a head for every passenger over 3 years old! In November 1875, the Khedive sold his shares in the canal (176,602 out of 400,000 ordinary) to the British Government for 3,976,582*l.*, but the interest upon them will not accrue to the country till 1894.

Ismailia, forty-four miles from Suez, is nearly the central point between Suez and Port Said, and overlooks Lake Timsah, one of the several bitter lakes, by which the canal is interrupted. The town has made its fortune by the canal, and is a convenient place to disembark with a view of spending a few days in Egypt, as it is connected by rail with Cairo through Tel-el-Kebir and Zagazig. Before the train draws up at the Tel-el-Kebir station, a low line of Arab earthworks in the sandy expanse still points out the scene of our victory in 1882, while a small cemetery, almost in the station, is the only other mark that remains of Lord Wolseley's engagement. Shortly afterwards, the burning desert is suddenly transformed into a fertile land of cotton, barley, and date-palms, dependent for its luxuriance upon the waters of the Nile. In the fields there is a division of labour between oxen, donkeys, and camels; a few horses are in use, but they are exceptional.

Cairo has nowadays become so fashionable and familiar that anything more than a passing notice of it will soon be as superfluous as a description of Paris. Its streets have of late become so modernised and full of traffic, so wide and well-paved, so crowded towards sunset with busy Arabs in their white turbans and loose blue dresses, or Egyptian gentlemen in a European get-up capped with a Turkish fez, so alive with donkeys and their riders, pressed on by drivers walking on foot behind, that the whole betrays a civilisation to which a traveller from the East has been quite unaccustomed. Even in the native quarter, the bazaars and shops look half-European, English or French being generally understood. But the flat roofs are peculiar, and so are most of the women, who are muffled over their heads and up to their eyes in black, and seem to be shortening their lives by a slow suffocation. Many of them wear on their foreheads a perpendicular ringed tube, which oriental taste presumes to be ornamental, and, as a rule, they go about the streets far more unreservedly than the Mahomedan women in India. The advertisements in Cairo are posted up in French, English, Greek, Italian, or Arabic.

The fine old mosque of Sultan Hassan, where the faint colourings on its lofty walls and arches bear testimony to its five centuries of existence, lies just at the foot of Saladin's citadel, still occupied—such is the irony of fate—by an army of British soldiery. At the citadel's summit is the great mosque of Mahomet Ali, conspicuous all over Cairo with its two slim, pointed minarets, and adorned round the dome inside with magnificent columns of alabaster. Elsewhere in the city and its neighbourhood, besides innumerable mosques and minarets, are the new Coptic churches,[1] the long and unpretentious Abdeen Palace, recently put up for the Khedive, and (not least) the strange Egyptian idols, mummies, stones, and hieroglyphics in the Boulak Museum.

[1] The Copts are the Egyptian Christians, and trace their descent from the original Egyptians. Their tenets, which are those of the ect called Jacobites, were pronounced heretical by the Council of Chalcedon in A.D. 581.

Of old Cairo, two or three miles away from the modern city, there remains little but a heap of ruins. The old Coptic churches, however, contain some venerable relics, and though terribly decayed are still employed for divine service. One of them, that of Abu Sirgeh, nine hundred years old, is built over a tiny subterranean chapel, held by tradition to have been the resting-place of the Holy Family after the flight into Egypt, and if this report is true, it is the greatest misfortune that the small church above it is allowed to waste away through the indifference or poverty of its pitiable congregation, six on Sundays, three on week-days. The cell-like chapel has plastered walls and pillars, and a basin or font, but it is without windows, and in three of its four walls there is a deep niche or seat, supposed to have been used by Our Lord and His Parents. The mosque of Amer, the conqueror of Egypt for the caliph Omar, is also in old Cairo. It is made prominent by an ill-repaired minaret over its gateway; and its neglected colonnades of grey marble pillars were very possibly stolen from the early Christian churches. A canal divides old Cairo from the island of Roda, now rumoured to be the spot where Moses was found by Pharaoh's daughter. At the near corner of the island, the ancient Nilometer still fulfils its annual work in measuring the rise of the Nile. It is a stone well some eighteen feet square, with a graduated stone pillar in the centre, and at the side it has two windows, one above the other, through which the Nile makes its way. It is inscribed with several bands of Cufic characters, carved in different places on its walls, and these seem to indicate that it is about a thousand years old. The maximum rise of the river at Cairo averages twenty-five feet.

Every Friday afternoon in Cairo, the Mahomedan Sunday is celebrated by the dancing and the howling dervishes. The former perform their active devotions before their sheik in a small circular mosque or convent, in the middle of which the best of dancing-floors is divided off by a wooden balustrade from the pavement of stones, upon which Europeans are allowed to stand, and above them is a screened gallery for Egyptian ladies, and a recess for discordant musicians. The dervishes, of whom there are generally about five-and-twenty, are dressed in long, unassuming cloaks and tall, sandy-coloured fezes, and after they have entered the dancing-stage, they seat themselves on mats at the edge of the floor for a short silent prayer, and then follow their sheik three times solemnly round the circle. When he returns to his mat, they begin one by one to dance, till all are engaged in pirouetting and twirling

before him, first for several minutes one way, and
then for several more the other, allowing themselves
only a few seconds to rest in between. The whole
of this giddy ceremonial lasts about half an hour.
The howling dervishes are even more perplexing.
Like the others, they perform in a mosque, but
they wear no particular dress, and stand all the
time in a circle. There they fling themselves
about in the wildest contortions, at the instance
of a leader in their centre, and accompany their
movements with a chorus of blasts, sometimes like
noisy steam-engines, sometimes like peals of thunder,
until at last their voices are drowned in a cannon-
roar of drums, which is the signal for them to
stop and regain breath before indulging in a fresh
outburst. A little singing occasionally soothes
their ardour, but there is no music, unless, indeed,
the drums may rank as such. The leaders distin-
guish themselves by wearing long hair, and are
always the more desperate fanatics, and it is not
hard to imagine that when such opponents with-
stood our troops in the Soudan, they utterly
scorned to accept the proffered quarter. All this
weekly exertion apparently aims at kneading their
brains into a supernatural dizziness which may
assist to withdraw their thoughts from all worldly
distractions. It must also set in motion a perfect
avalanche of extravagant whims.

To a spectator at Cairo, the pyramids of Ghizeh (so called from the name of the district round them), are always dimmed by a burning haze. These marvels of prehistoric times, the illustrious vanities of bygone tyranny, have a form too familiar to be insulted by description, indeed their pictures have been with most of us childhood acquaintances. They are a ten-mile drive out of Cairo, along a capital road which crosses the Nile on a fine iron bridge, and is afterwards shaded by an avenue of acacias, and bordered by irrigated fields. It is usual to visit the Sphinx first, by wading from the great pyramid a quarter of a mile through the sand. His human face and lion's body are carved out of the solid sandstone rock, and his huge paws, which have the appearance of worn brick, but are really painted stones, have been much excavated so lately as 1886. In his prime, he was probably a local deity. His face is 18 feet long, and he measures about 60 feet from the top of his head to the bottom of his paws; his body is 102 feet long, and he is perhaps even older than the pyramids. Near him a temple has been dug out very recently, where the great pillars and walls of red granite, once floated down from the first cataract, look so smooth and perfect, that they might well have been chiselled yesterday; and at no great distance the ruined causeway can still be traced, over which the pyramid-stones were brought from a quarry on the Cairo side of the Nile. Wandering back to the pyramids, there are three large ones, all at least 40 centuries old, and several smaller ones and tombs; the great pyramid of King Cheops, built by himself to inter his own remains, being the nearest to Cairo, and the farthest the smallest of the three. The pyramid of Cheops is the tallest in Egypt, and its approximate measurements are quite astounding—no wonder that it occupied 100,000 men for 30 years, and ranked among the seven wonders of the world! Its base is about 740 feet square, and it is now 460 feet high,[1] or 610 feet along its slope of limestone steps. These steps, which are each 2 to 5 or 6 feet high, are cemented together, and were formerly filled in, so as to make a smooth slanting surface like that which still exists at the top of the second pyramid. With the 460 feet of the great pyramid, it is interesting to compare other well-known heights. Strasburg Cathedral is 468 feet high; the dome of St. Peter's at Rome is 429 feet; and Salisbury Cathedral is 404 feet high : St. Paul's in London is only 356 feet high. But its height cannot be treated with indifference

---

[1] Its height was originally 480ft. 9in., but it has been much impaired.

after climbing it ; an ambition (it is true) with no possible object, except to say that one has been to the top, and so exhaustive that it is more than gratified on being accomplished once in a lifetime. Every climber sets to work, whether he likes it or not, with three Bedouin Arabs, belonging to some of these wandering tribes, whose sheiks are deputed by the Government to protect the pyramids, and to check (if they do not connive at) the cheating to which visitors are exposed; but even with their help it is not easy to scale a slope of 610 feet, composed of steps averaging a height of about 4 feet ; and it is a vicarious and decidedly preferable amusement to watch an Arab run up and down them in eight or nine minutes. For oneself, if one is so desperate as to climb, it is a great triumph to reach the panorama at the top, perhaps a greater one to be back safely at the bottom, and the expedition is only spoilt by the constant demands for 'backsheesh,' which are here even more persistent and crafty than the plaintive moans in India. All Arabs are nations of beggars, who only care for foreigners as a species of dummy, created for disgorging mines of gold. The first word their little urchins learn is 'back sheesh;' the murmur, we believe, is the same from an old man on his deathbed. The atmosphere inside the pyramids is terribly stuffy, and there is little to see; but their grim beauty is very enjoyable by moonlight.

Another drive from Cairo is that to the old site of Heliopolis, where there is a fine red granite obelisk, which is deeply carved with large hieroglyphics. It is a monolith 62 feet high, and is the oldest in Egypt, since the king whose name it bears (Osirtasen I.) reigned at least 4,000 years ago.

Near this road, modern speculators have established an ostrich farm, five miles in circumference, and capable of maintaining about six hundred ostriches, which are kept in sandy enclosures of mud walls, and fed mostly on ship-biscuit. Many are hatched in incubators, and the birds range from a few days to eight years old. They are said to live upwards of thirty. The process of plucking them is asserted to be a painless one, and should be performed once a year, in March or April; but they resist and kick freely, and it requires fifteen Arabs to pluck a single bird. The best feathers are sold wholesale in Europe, at four or five francs apiece.

Till the end of March it is possible to go up the Nile twelve miles at least from Cairo to Bedreshayn, but by that time the water is getting very shallow, and a steamer encounters many sand-banks, of which it has to steer clear. From

Bedreshayn it is about two hours' donkey-ride to the village and eleven pyramids of Sakkárah, and towards spring, a traveller is lucky if he avoids any sudden onset of the fearful 'Khamseen' wind. Much of the road lies through the desert; and on such an occasion this fiery blast only intensifies the already piercing blaze of the sun and the binding glare which is reflected by the sand; and it may easily be imagined that its withering heat can scorch up the enjoyment of even the most ardent tourist. The way to Sakkárah leads past the ruins of Memphis, where only a few stones and substructures are left to represent its fossil greatness; while close by there is a colossal stone statue of Rameses II., lying on its back, as well as a smaller companion vaguely intended for transportation to the British Museum. The eleven pyramids at Sakkárah are at considerable intervals from each other; perhaps the most curious, though not the most handsome, is one constructed in the shape of five enormous steps, which rather accentuate than improve its ruined condition. Intersected by subterranean passages are the twenty-four tombs of Sakkárah, each one distinguishable by a granite sarcophagus, and all arranged in rows throughout a long vault or cave: the tomb of Tih is a separate underground room at some distance from them, artistically decorated with very well-preserved specimens of Egyptian pictures and hieroglyphics. Half a mile away, in the interior of the small pyramid of Ounas, there are also very perfect hieroglyphical inscriptions, and another granite sarcophagus is imprisoned in the last of its little cells. On riding back to Bedreshayn, excursionists can return to Cairo either by water or by rail.

With two or three months to spend in Egypt, and both river and thermometer at a normal height, nothing could be more agreeable than a trip far up the Nile to Thebes, Luxor, and Assouan. But the hurried wanderer must be content to speed on to Alexandria, and forego for the time such tempting attractions.

From an antiquarian point of view, modern Alexandria is an uninteresting city. Everyone goes to see Pompey's Pillar, which was not put up to him at all, but was really in honour of Diocletian, and formerly everyone used to visit Cleopatra's Needle, which by Mahomet Ali's generosity has now come to enrich the Thames Embankment at home. But the town is a busy one, and the harbour especially so, with its steamers, and sailing-vessels, passengers, and merchandise. Rain seldom falls: perhaps on an average it pours a dozen times a year —and at Cairo a storm is scarcely known. From the mouth of the bay the view of Alexandria is very comprehensive, embracing on the left its ungainly modern lighthouse and the Khedive's palace, and being flanked on the right by the stubborn Mex forts, which endured a heavy share of our bombardment in 1882.

And here, at last, with the departure from Alexandria, this tour round the world comes practically to an end; and half its pleasure must always be that of returning home. A choice is open between several routes back to England, the shortest being through Brindisi or Marseilles; but in either case the Mediterranean must be challenged, and the risk run of a squall on its blue and fickle waves. There is a bleak authenticity in the breezes and clouds of Europe, which is none the less extremely welcome; while a few palms, aloe hedges, and prickly pears are the sole isolated adventurers whose hardiness has braved the winters of our northern shores. In France the national blouse picturesquely recalls one's approach nearer home, and even the Paris *canaille* has its recommendations over the importunities of Arab beggars. Eight hours—so we are told by the sanguine continental time-bills—are sufficient to bridge over the distance between Paris and London, and to launch the wayfarer once more into the uncertainties of an English climate. Notwithstanding its abuse, it still holds its own against weathers in all parts of the world (excepting, perhaps, California), and it is at least less enervating than the feverish blaze of the tropics and the weary cloudlessness of an Indian sky.

A journey round the world is a pleasure never to be regretted, and teems at every step with experiences as instructive as they are interesting. It incites a lasting interest in the pithy newspaper paragraphs, which circulate every morning the latest information from countries which have been visited, and it teaches once for all the invaluable lesson that there are other places and other customs besides those so precious to dear, busy little England.

www.ingramcontent.com/pod-product-compliance
Lightning Source LLC
Chambersburg PA
CBHW020801230426
43666CB00007B/792